"WHOLLY UN-ACCEPTABLE"

"WHOLLY UN-ACCEPTABLE"

The Bitter Battle for Sotheby's

JEFFREY HOGREFE

WILLIAM MORROW
AND COMPANY, INC.
NEW YORK

Library of Congress Cataloging-in-Publication Data

Hogrefe, Jeffrey.
"Wholly unacceptable."

Includes index.
1. Sotheby's (Firm)   2. Auctions.   3. Art
auctions.   I. Title.
HF5477.G74S6743   1986   381'.1   85-29836
ISBN 0-688-02918-3

Printed in the United States of America

First Edition

1 2 3 4 5 6 7 8 9 10

BOOK DESIGN BY JAYE ZIMET

To my grandfather John Beck Fullen (1901–1978)

ACKNOWLEDGMENTS

SO many people helped with the preparation of this book that it is impossible to name them all, but particular thanks must go to David Bathurst, Elizabeth Furse, John Herbert, Isolde McNicholl, Robert Miller, Daniel Moynihan, Stephanie Pereire, and David Yudain. Without their help this book would not have been possible in its present form.

I would also like to thank especially John Marion of Sotheby's, and Marshall Cogan and Stephen Swid. Their aid in re-creating the various private phone conversations and boardroom meetings throughout the book was indispensable.

Special thanks to Mary Evans and Virginia Barber for their encouragement and support.

Most of all to Douglas Stumpf, my editor, without whom this book would not have been possible in any form. I am forever grateful.

PROLOGUE

I NVITATIONS to Sotheby's annual spring auction of the most valuable paintings in the world were issued weeks beforehand. But had anyone foreseen what would happen the evening of May 18, 1983, the two thousand tickets would have vanished even sooner.

Auction. The very word suggests the unknown, a festival of free enterprise unhindered by all but the most basic regulations. Here is a gentleman's game rooted in antiquity, designed to activate the sporting blood in elite gatherings of the worldly and wealthy.

There is, to be sure, precedent for dramatic auctions; one of the most notable took place during the decline of the Roman Empire. In A.D. 193 the rich senator Marcus Didius Julianus won the entire empire at an auction. He bought it from the Praetorian Guard, a band of thugs whose dubious claim to the moribund ancient world was secured through force: They had assassinated duly elected Emperor Pertinax. Julianus immediately proclaimed himself emperor, but he had a rough time asserting his ownership. His sixty-six-day reign ended when a mob beheaded him in public.

Nothing this spectacular would happen tonight, but it gives you an idea of how emotional auctions can be, particularly in times of great flux. This sale begins as evening sales in New York have begun each May and November since Sotheby's—a 239-year-old London-based auction house with close ties to the crown—merged with New York's Parke-Bernet Galleries in 1964. Evening sales were banned in London until 1958 and in New York until a few years later, primarily because auctioneers could not be trusted after the sun descended in the West. But now they are the main events of the year.

Sotheby's lean ultramodern salesroom hums with the sound of wallets opening and closing. Outside, black limousines idle knee-deep by the curb like so many getaway cars in a heist thriller, Cadillacs and Mercedeses outnumbering Lincolns and Rollses two to one. The equal proportion of gray-haired moguls to blond *jeunes filles* is noticeable, many of the latter being second wives and paramours plucked from Sotheby's and archrival Christie's decorous staff of pretty women with perfect noses and a way of talking that involves very little jaw motion. Those still hoping hand out catalogs to the gathering throng or check credit references and dispense bright-green round plastic bidding paddles to those who qualify. Each name becomes a number, but some faces betray their owners: Banker David Rockefeller leads the pack with a seat in the first of some sixty rows (twenty seats across) in the main salesroom. Nearby is Donald Marron, the president of brokerage house Paine Webber. In a burst of strobe lights, California industrialist and museum founder Norton Simon enters the house on the arm of his wife, Jennifer Jones, the former movie star.

This being America, where fortunes come and go quickly, a number of victors in the latest round on Wall Street are here, too, jostling each other like dignitaries who have not learned protocol, flexing their muscles in the oligarchy that rules America in the 1980s. Socialites, entertainers, and assorted demimondaines have turned out.

Providing the sweet airs of perfume at $500 an ounce and hairdos out to here for distraction are Elisabeth of Yugoslavia, who would be queen of the Balkan nation had not Stalin claimed it (now she is merely the mother of *Dynasty* star Catherine Oxenberg), socialites Pat Buckley and Nan Kempner, and designer Paloma Picasso. Jack Nicholson, Paul Simon, and Steve Martin provide celluloid faces for identification. Nicholson slides his trademark dark glasses coyly down his nose to acknowledge a friend. Those with no cachet watch the sale via closed-circuit television in a room to the side.

Most of these people will not bid. Sotheby's, of course, will gladly do the bidding for you, either over a phone hookup or through an agent provided by the house. They are here because art auctions are to the twentieth century what watching the king eat was to the eighteenth, a place to be seen and a chance to see a spectacle: grown men and women spending more money than most see in a lifetime for something no one needs. Tonight's sale is a scorecard in brief for the current battle for social prestige. Ownership of works of art, especially expensive ones that could be in museums, separates the men from the boys today, much as gifts to the church or loyalty to a crown once distinguished the arriviste from the aristocrat. Sotheby's and Christie's are where the action is. The salesroom adds excitement—the crinkle of well-fitting taffeta gowns, the sparkle of flawless diamonds and emeralds the size of Ping-Pong balls, the futile rush of vast sums of money in the face of great beauty—to an otherwise cerebral activity, the understanding and appreciation of art.

Rigged out in dinner jackets and black tie, the senior officers of the auction house line the front of the room in solemn deference to the occasion. The fifteenth earl of Westmorland—who as Master of the Horse rides before Queen Elizabeth II in royal processions and who as chairman of the board until recently held the reins at Sotheby's—greets friends and clients. His cousin Peter Wilson, chairman emeritus and architect of the modern auction spectacle, stands like an old soldier at the front of the room. Gracefully tailored, with a narrow black silk tie knotted like the Duke of Windsor's below his chiseled pink Anglo-Saxon face, Wilson commands the room as though he were about to mount the podium.

But the auctioneer this night is John Marion, president of

Sotheby's enormously successful American division. A six-foot 190-pound all-American type of Irish and Italian descent, he presents sharp contrast to the tony British upper management. From the rear of the beige auditorium-size room, Marion looks like a TV game-show emcee, with his loose-fitting dinner jacket, butterfly bow tie, and full head of dark-brown hair in spite of his fifty years. A thin brown More cigarette dangles on his lower lip, à la Clint Eastwood in *Dirty Harry*. His tough-smooth voice, accented with New Yorkisms, can be heard testing the microphone behind the mahogany Chippendale podium.

Although he knows less about works of art than many collectors, Marion knows how to conduct an auction. He may embarrass the firm with egregious gaffes, like the time he told a reporter that the reason Sotheby's had fallen on bad times was that "death has been bad to us," or the time he told a group at lunch that the firm had gone into the business of auctioning Thoroughbreds, when in fact the horse sale in Arizona was of Arabian stallions; the British may call him a cowboy and he may despise them for their condescension, but behind the podium the man comes to life. He has a sense of drama, an unflinching cool in the face of million-dollar bidding battles. There is good reason for John Marion to be called America's favorite art auctioneer. And anyway, he is one of Sotheby's largest shareholders.

The successful marriage of British polish with American showmanship has been one of Sotheby's great achievements in the postwar period. Banking on the rampant Anglophilia in America—which filters down even to the level of heraldic devices on the side of mail-order thimbles, and mock-Tudor shopping centers in suburbia—Sotheby's has taught America how to collect, or at least claims to have. And the comforting thing about the firm is the nice American fellow—"just like us"—called John Marion, who will greet you at the door.

Sotheby's is British. The British are honorable, gentlemanly businessmen. So the thinking goes, not least of all among the upper tiers of America's monied class. Being called Sotheby's (pronounced SUH-thu-bees) makes life easier for agents of other people's misfortunes—like death and bankruptcy.

The main event tonight is the result of a death: sixteen paintings from the estate of Doris Dick Havemeyer. Havemeyer, as the sale is called, even though it also includes some seventy pictures from other consignors, is quite a name in American art and money circles. As the daughter-in-law of the famous nineteenth-century sugar baron Henry O. Havemeyer, the late Doris Dick was guardian of a fabled assembly of mostly French Impressionist and post-Impressionist artworks. The founding Havemeyers—H.O., his wife Louisine Waldron, and good friend Mary Cassatt, the artist—purchased Renoirs and Degases and Monets by the yard, fresh from the easel, much as H.O. purchased sugar by the boatload. On H.O.'s death in the 1930s, much of the collection went to the Metropolitan Museum of Art in New York where it formed the backbone of the museum's holdings in this field.

By the time Doris Dick died in 1982, what with cost-of-living increases, death duties, and other money-sapping ailments of old money in the United States, all that was left of the once-fabled assembly were these sixteen. There may have been superior Corots, Manets, Renoirs, and Degases on the market, but only these carried the Havemeyer name. Sotheby's, as any good art dealer would have, exploited the name fully. The concept is as brilliant as it is simple: Take the pictures of a well-known industrialist, tycoon, or otherwise rich person and put them in a handsome clothbound catalog with that person's name on the sleeve. Play down the pictures; play up the name.

These are not just oil paintings and pastels. They belonged to a benefactor of the Metropolitan Museum of Art. Never mind that the fabled Havemeyer eye could hardly err buying canvases by the crateload. Never mind that no major museum today would call this assembly a collection. Though there are a few superb Degas pastels and a sparkling Monet of a Dutch seaport, the Havemeyer name would boost the value of more than half the sixteen artworks. Havemeyer was a peer of Mellon, Frick, Gould, a member of the gilded group of robber barons who lived before income tax and the Securities and Exchange Commission. These pictures are what rich men want—Guccis for the walls.

While many bidders scramble to find seats as Marion opens contest on the first lot, others are already raising their paddles. Bids fly through the room, as though out of thin air, first from this corner, then through an agent via one of the red phone hookups in the front—all reflected on a digital currency-conversion board, like a scoreboard in a baseball game, next to the revolving stage. Click, click, click—as soon as you can say one thousand dollars, a new figure appears on the board, in dollars, deutschmarks, yen, French francs, Swiss francs, for the benefit of those bidding in foreign money, of which there are more than a few.

A quick rap of the hammer. "Number two forty-three." Marion calls out a bidder's paddle number and the price he has paid for the tiny Degas. At $65,000 the landscape has fetched nearly twice the generally accepted estimate, or double what any dealer could have asked for it. When it works, the auction system works beautifully. Sotheby's 10 percent buyer's premium brings the price tag to $71,500.

Ten minutes later and the audience is finally quiet. Everyone has found a seat and greeted neighbors, friends, prospective competitors. Marion has knocked down seven pictures, nearly half the Havemeyer estate, each one bringing a sum that bears no relationship to the estimate in the catalog. Bidding on lot number eight begins at $1 million. "L'Attante" is a tiny Degas pastel, this one of a mother and her ballerina daughter working out at the barre. When Degas painted the picture in 1897, according to the catalog entry, he sold it to the dealer who sold it to the Havemeyers for $90.

A woman in the twelfth row wants the picture badly. She announces her intention to go for the finish by holding her green paddle skyward. In bold defiance of generally accepted auction strategy, she refuses to lower the paddle between bids. Bids climb rapidly, in $100,000 increments, passing $2 million in seconds rather than minutes. The sound of money fills the room like water over a spillway, drowning all other thoughts, rendering all preconceived notions of value and prudence obsolete. Draped in a white chiffon togalike outfit, the mystery contestant looks like the Statue of Liberty holding out her torch to oncoming ships,

and everyone stretches to see who she is. Within seconds the
room buzzes with recognition.

The woman in the twelfth row who is just now bidding $2
million for the tiny pastel (not even an oil) is Jennifer Jones,
Oscar-winning star of the 1948 *Song of Bernadette*. The audience bursts into applause. Marion beams proudly from behind
the Chippendale podium. Jones, who basically retired from acting
before she became Mrs. Norton Simon, clearly enjoys her brief
comeback. Clutching her triple strand of pearls, she forms a
petite moue with her lips and thrusts the paddle skyward for
more bidding: $2.1 million, $2.2 million, $2.3 million, $2.4 million. Quicker than you can say five, six, seven, eight, nine, the
contest stops suddenly at $3 million. The audience applauds and
applauds. The room vibrates.

Sitting next to Jones is husband Simon, a self-made college
dropout who parlayed a $7,000 investment into a billion-dollar
food conglomerate under his name. He has said that he suffers
greatly "in the Dostoevskian sense." Forbes put his net worth
at $100 million-plus when he sold out in 1969. Since then it has
mushroomed to $200 million-plus, mostly through art invest-
ments, including a museum in Pasadena under his name. Sur-
prisingly, Simon takes over the bidding from his wife. Using
secret prearranged signals, he drives the hammer price to $3.7
million.

Later on, Jack Nicholson successfully bids for a Matisse still
life. But for most people the highlight of the evening is the
comeback of Jennifer Jones. The sight of the aging actress and
ashen seventy-six-year-old food mogul fleeing the salesroom under the gaze of television cameras from around the world will
remain fixed in their minds. Nothing like this has ever happened before. The bravura was staggering. Imagine letting his
wife take the bidding up to $3 million, only to finish the round
when the stakes got tough.

The auction room does strange things to people. Sotheby's,
above all. A small firm in the world of multinationals, founded
in 1744 so gentlemen could exchange property without unseemly face-to-face haggling, Sotheby's is this very night in the
midst of one of the most unseemly take-over battles in the his-

tory of corporate piracy. There is not much money involved, a mere $100 million or so. But there is much teeth gnashing on both sides of the Atlantic. Sotheby's has strong symbolic meaning for reasons only partially clear right now. At the moment, either Prime Minister Margaret Thatcher or Queen Elizabeth II, depending on whom you ask, has blocked the bid in the eleventh hour. The bid would wrest the house from British hands to those of two Americans, perceived as "unacceptable felt merchants." Some people now are wondering if Simon will be the much-rumored American White Knight on the way to save the damsel Sotheby's, or if there is a White Knight, as Sotheby's has promised.

PART I

GENTLEMAN'S AGREEMENT

ONE

PETER Wilson slipped off his hand-sewn soft leather loafers (ordered at considerable expense from a small shop off Jermyn Street in London) and pulled on the soft blue felt slippers Air France provides passengers aboard the Concorde.

The Paris-bound jet took off with a quick jolt. Once it reached cruising altitude, Wilson slowly closed his eyes and thought back to the Havemeyer sale. *Once again*, he proudly thought, I *made things click*.

Wilson may not have been thought powerful anymore. Marion, after all, had conducted the sale. All that Wilson had done was stand in front of the room, noting prices and buyers in his elegant script in the clothbound catalog. Wilson had not even met with the press after the sale, an activity he had relished over the years. To most in the room, he had appeared to be an old and distinguished English gentleman, soigné, soft-spoken, a bit shy in spite of his commanding (six foot four inch) height and broad-shouldered build, like Sir John Gielgud playing a slightly decadent antiques dealer.

Distinguished, in a word. He was the perfect leader for Sotheby's. Central casting could not have come up with a bet-

ter one. Never mind that he hadn't always behaved like a
gentleman.

Under Wilson's tireless direction Sotheby's became one of
the few notable success stories of postwar Britain. He turned
the auction world on its head and dusted off its dull image by
combining the genteel excitement of a top-drawer Monte Carlo
gambling casino with the promotion machinery of a Hollywood
studio in the thirties. Under his direction from 1958 to 1979,
Sotheby's proved that "the price of art will always go up," as
he himself liked to say, over and over. Even after he suddenly
stepped down in 1979 he devised ways to run the firm and took
credit for every success.

It wasn't his fault that he was forced to retire. Everyone
knew that. Or at least he thought they knew. As a man who had
grown rich through the art market, he had to be concerned about
estate taxes in Great Britain. By moving his residence to France,
he sought to avoid British death duties. After all, he had two
sons to think about. Plenty of other Englishmen had done it,
particularly during the Labour government years in Britain when
taxation reached the all-time ridiculous rates of 100 percent of
income in the upper levels. He had always liked the South of
France, and always said he would one day retire to his estate
outside Grasse, a few miles inland from Cannes and the Côte
d'Azur.

He was, to be sure, defensive about his decision. Sotheby's
suffered greatly after he departed. By British law he became a
nonresident tax exile and was allowed to reside in Britain only
sixty days a year. It was impossible for him to run Sotheby's
on sixty days a year. He had tried to run it through his cousin
Lord Westmorland. But that was a fiasco. Westmorland was incapable of modern management. He is very nice and very
charming—but ineffectual. Even he admits he is, and claims he
asked Wilson to find someone else. He was the only one, Wilson
would claim.

The situation was only made worse by Wilson's stock sale.
As a publicly traded *private limited company*, or p.l.c. in British trading parlance, shares in Sotheby's climbed very quickly
for the first two years. Then Wilson left and began to sell his

shares. Other directors followed suit; a few others sold out completely when Wilson passed over them to make Westmorland chairman. All of which made Sotheby's as vulnerable to a take-over as a featherless duck. Shares were simply too widespread to block anyone from taking the place for his own.

Then there were the rumors. Englishmen suddenly retiring to the South of France generally start some talk. There is good reason for Graham Greene to have called the area "a very sunny place for very shady Englishmen," but Wilson's departure only fueled the rumors that he was among the shadiest, as most of the small and fastidious art world would realize in the years after he resigned.

Small wonder then that Wilson would run to his beloved Château de Clavary whenever he could. For there in the Mediterranean hills, hidden behind an alley of pine trees, on a ten-acre parklike ground with a coral-lined swimming pool the size of a pond, he inhabited his own world in the blazing sun. The checks from Sotheby's still arrived regularly. Aside from a small salary, he also received various commissions for sales he brought in. Not to mention well-placed sales of items from his extensive art and antiques collection. If anyone knew how to trade in works of art, it was Peter Cecil Wilson.

When people spoke of Sotheby's as Wilson's creation, they of course did not mean he had started the place. Sotheby's was founded thirty-two years before the American Revolution on the simple premise that one man's dross is another's treasure. Along with archrival Christie's, it served the upper class along school ties, business from Harrovians going to Sotheby's while Etonians "sent things down for sale" at Christie's. Eton being for the most part snappier and richer than Harrow, Christie's prospered while Sotheby's struggled—a victim, as it were, of the class system.

There was generally enough business, though, for both auction houses. As well as the standard death and bankruptcy troubles, the two London-based houses benefited from every imaginable blow to wealth. Governments would rise. Governments would fall. Fortunes were made. Fortunes were squandered. No matter what happened, Sotheby's and Christie's stood to benefit, coming and going. Following the French Revolution, boatloads of furnishings crossed the English Channel to the auction block. Although few people bother to think about it, many of the so-called great houses of England, like the Marlboroughs' Blenheim Palace as well as the Windsors' Buckingham Palace, are more French, at least in style, than English. Upheavals in Germany and Italy, later in the Balkans, and of course the 1917 Bolshevik Revolution in Russia, further enriched Sotheby's and Christie's coffers. Britain during the reign of Victoria was, it seemed, one of the few safe ports in Western Europe.

Britain was also a discreet place to do business, and few institutions were as discreet as Sotheby's and Christie's. Acting as independent agent on behalf of the buyer and seller, the resident curator would cautiously advertise His Grace's silver coupe as "property of a gentleman." Only those who had been for the weekend might recognize the piece. Even if they did, they probably would not admit it. To admire—or even recognize—silver or works of art in philistine England is generally avoided; to do so would reveal a womanly deficiency few Englishmen outside Oscar Wilde or the Duke of Windsor could carry off.

Granted, property of a gentleman would sometimes turn out to be property of a thief. The system of discretion had its drawbacks and over the years safeguards were devised to protect both the selling and buying public. The success of the safeguards depended on the honesty of the resident catalogers employed by the firms. For it was their task to compile a brief history of the piece or picture, including the provenance, previous owners (particularly famous people and institutions), exhibitions, passages in scholarly books mentioning it, and any other means of establishing the credibility of the piece. The seller may remain anonymous, but the history was supposed to be checked and if possible revealed to prospective buyers. Or so the thinking went. Of course there were cases when stolen goods surfaced on the auction market, though serious art thieves tended to operate in Italy, Switzerland or Monte Carlo, where title passes unquestioned from seller to buyer.

The salesrooms chose their staffs from the upper class,

where careers were made generally in the public service industries, either in the City in banking or in Westminster in the
government; both Sotheby's and Christie's were popular for those
interested in the arts. People of course make money in banking, gain power in the government, but why they would choose
a career in the auction houses remains a mystery on the surface. Perhaps it is the intrigue. Perhaps it is the glamour. Perhaps it is the only place for sensitive intellectuals interested in
the arts. Or perhaps for some the auction houses provide money
and a certain sort of power. This allure remains a mystery to
most. Thackeray considered the salesrooms "full of odious snobs
and bombazine women." Oscar Wilde said that the auctioneer
"knows the price of everything and the value of nothing." Modern-day *Private Eye* has called the salesroom "a load of old
rubbish" and dubbed Christie's "Upper Chrusties"; Sotheby's,
"Knomby's."

Take the case of Peter Cecil Wilson. Born in 1913 the third
son of a conservative Victorian baronet, young Wilson had no
idea what he wanted to do when he came of an age to do something. As third son in a country ruled by primogeniture Wilson
would not inherit title or estate from his parents. Having finished his course at Eton and read history at New College, Oxford, young Wilson faced the world unprepared for the grim
Depression of 1932. Like many sensitive fair-haired English boys
at odds with their parents and the old fashion mores left over
from Victoria, young Wilson wanted to speak French like a
Frenchman. Sir Matthew, the fourth baronet, and Lady Wilson, his wife, the daughter of the great sportsman Lord Ribblesdale, were appalled by the idea. Maintaining that Paris was
too decadent, they finally accepted the idea of a French-speak-
ing son and sent young Peter to Geneva. They may speak French
there, his parents probably reasoned, but at least they don't
think like Frenchmen.

Sir Matthew and Lady Wilson would probably have been
surprised to learn their third son had found decadence at home
in England before he even set foot on the Continent. While at
Oxford, Wilson was befriended by Guy Burgess, a self-pro-
claimed homosexual who would later shock the nation—and free

world—not by his preference for men but by his preference for
the Soviet Union. Burgess was a spy for the Soviets working in
the British establishment. It was, granted, a time of much political confusion. Leading intellectuals of the day were almost
forced to choose sides. Between Stalin on the one hand and Hitler
on the other, it is hard to say in hindsight whether there was a
right decision. Wilson appears to have been apolitical, but he
was active in the Burgess circle.

Once in Geneva, Wilson expanded his network of interesting friends. There he met Pepi Lederer, Marion Davies's niece.
Lederer was in Geneva under the aegis of Davies's paramour
and supporter, William Randolph Hearst. W.R. supported not
only Davies but also her immediate family and close friends,
including her niece Pepi. Until Louise Brooks's autobiographi-
cal *Lulu in Hollywood,* few people knew the real story of the
girl whom Wilson called "my friend Pepi Lederer," or why she
committed suicide in 1935. Brooks seems to believe "being Marion
Davies' niece was one of the reasons, and Marion's being the
mistress of William Randolph Hearst was probably another."
Brooks mourned her as a talented but misguided soul adrift in
Hollywood, New York, and London with only cocaine and a girl
friend, Monica Morris (who was dubbed the Stage Door Ferret
because she was one of Tallulah Bankhead's groupies) to keep
her happy.

Wilson was enraptured by Lederer and the Stage Door
Ferret. "I *adored* Pepi," he said fondly, "and her friend Monica. They introduced me to a world I had never known to exist
. . . the world of Hearst and Hollywood . . . the world of the
stage and of opulent living. She was so much fun!"

After he had read the account of Lederer in *Lulu in Hollywood,* Wilson changed his story. "I really didn't know her very
well at all . . . at all. You understand that, don't you?"

Wilson's first "real" job was on *The Connoisseur.* Lederer
had arranged the job for him, and he was so proud of it "because neither my family nor their friends had anything to do
with it. I was so happy in my independence and my new life
[outside his family]. And my parents were proud of me. *The
Connoisseur* was a respected publication."

Within a year, though, Wilson had grown disenchanted with his new life on *The Connoisseur*. The job Lederer had arranged for him was in the business department of the quarterly: He sold advertising space to art galleries and antiques dealers. In the middle of the Great Depression, which had dragged on into 1936, selling anything became increasingly difficult. Business at the auction houses was better than most places. People wanted to sell and the Depression barely dented the purses of the super-rich buyers. By the end of 1937, Wilson had become an assistant cataloger at Sotheby's, one of his main accounts from *The Connoisseur*.

Wilson wasn't sure at first that he liked Sotheby's either. Being a snob—as well as an Etonian—he felt he belonged at Christie's. Moreover, by his own admission, he knew little about art or antiques—"not even the difference between Chippendale and Louis XVI"—and he wasn't sure he wanted to learn. His first Sotheby's boss may have been a "complete autocrat" who made life "difficult," but "One couldn't be too picky during the Depression," Wilson concluded and set out to learn about art and antiques, beginning with antique furniture. With his background, he was a welcome addition to the staff at Sotheby's. It was felt—and still is—that young men from good families would bring more property in for sale.

Within a few months Wilson discovered not only that he had the right background for the auction field, but that he actually enjoyed it. Through the generous gifts of a photographic memory and acute sense of style that would serve him well throughout his life, he became one of the senior staff in no time at all. Before the war abruptly ended his civilian life, he had risen to head of the furniture division on New Bond Street in Mayfair.

For Wilson the war opened new vistas: In 1940 he was admitted into MI-5, the British equivalent of the American CIA. MI-5 was primarily comprised of men and women—like Wilson—from good families and good schools. For Wilson, who served alongside Donald Maclean and Kim Philby in Washington, MI-5 was "the most exciting period of my life."

Exactly what he found so exciting has never been made

clear. Obviously much of the goings on of a secret service are meant to be kept secret, and when asked he would respond with characteristic discretion. He would say that he worked closely with the news media in Washington and that he benefited from watching Americans close up. "I decided then and there that the future of the world was in America." This was not a novel idea given the times, but one that was perhaps new to the hide-bound British art world. Following the war Wilson continued to pursue a career in military intelligence. Finally in 1947 he was persuaded to return to Sotheby's, again for reasons he would not divulge. "I did it with great reservations," was all he would say.

After the intrigue and glamour of MI-5, life at Sotheby's seemed dull. Once again he had little choice in the matter. The postwar period in Britain was bleak and jobless; a man like Wilson, with a wife and two small children, had to take whatever jobs were available. Wilson, the Sotheby's man, as he became known during this period, spent nearly all his waking hours at New Bond Street. Not that there was much to sell in the reconstruction era—many great houses had been bombed by the Nazis, and in fact, Christie's suffered a direct hit during the war and was closed for several years.

Before long, Wilson was Sotheby's, and Sotheby's was Wilson. Colleagues remember his calling them from home as early as six in the morning to discuss matters that could have waited until normal business hours. By 1958 he had ascended to the presidency. At that time he also began his love affair with the South of France in earnest. He bought a small stucco redoubt on the beach at Saint-Tropez. It was the heyday of the Côte d'Azur, with Brigitte Bardot and Grace Kelly, not to mention Somerset Maugham, setting the tone. Wilson spent every possible free moment there.

TWO

JUDGING from photographs alone, yellow and faded though they may be a quarter century later, the 1958 Goldschmidt auction was quite a do.

The war was a faint memory for most. Prosperity had returned to the Western world—with a vengeance—and the crowd outside Sotheby's New Bond Street salesroom looked impressively well-heeled.

Peter Wilson would change auction history this night. He would do so by mating commerce and theater in a grand display of avarice and showmanship. And if anyone doubts this, one has merely to glance at the guest list. Leading the select 1,500 were Dame Margot Fonteyn, Kirk Douglas, Anthony Quinn, writer Somerset Maugham, millionaires Paul Mellon, Henry Ford II, and wealthy expatriate Florence Gould, the lusty widow of Frank Jay Gould whose spending habits would make her a legend in her own time.

The headlines the next day read SOTHEBY'S SETS NEW RECORD IN ART SALES! Painting after painting had exceeded even the most generous expectations. The willingness to spend knew no bounds and Wilson took advantage of the situation. Few could see through his cool and imperturbable facade. But in the moments before the sale, as the elegant crowd settled into the padded folding seats of Sotheby's main salesroom and television crews lined the walls with their cameras and cables, Wilson was nervous—extremely so. The Goldschmidt sale was a gamble, a big gamble in a world where gambles occur daily, where the bottom could fall out at the blink of an eye. And Wilson knew this better than anyone else.

He also knew that he had to take risks. He had to take risks because it was the only way to overtake archrival Christie's. The odds were in Christie's favor, for Christie's controlled most of the estates of Britain's great aristocratic families. These people rarely bargain creatively and almost never change spending or buying habits. *So be it*, Wilson thought. Sotheby's, beginning with the Goldschmidt sale, would look to America.

The seed for the idea had been planted in Wilson during his early years. The example of Pepi Lederer and the merry spending Hearsts had impressed him greatly. His stint in Washington under MI-5 had further enhanced his view of America as a land of boundless wealth. America after the war was even more attractive. Added to the great robber-baron fortunes formed before the wars were the great Jewish fortunes from Central and Eastern Europe. German Jews like the late Jakob Goldschmidt—and, most important for Sotheby's, their art collections—had found refuge from Nazism and Communism in the United States.

A Berlin banker who fled Nazi Germany shortly after *Kristallnacht* in 1937, Goldschmidt typified the type of collector Wilson so avidly sought. Before he was forced to become a refugee, Goldschmidt controlled a sizable fortune, including one of the leading collections of twentieth-century art in Germany. Like most exiles, he was forced to depart quickly, leaving behind nearly all his money and most of his collection. By 1945, after struggling against the worst odds for Jews since the Middle Ages, Goldschmidt had remade much of his fortune and formed a new collection of Impressionist and modern paintings.

There was one problem that pained the banker greatly. With his newly acquired wealth, he could reconstruct his collection, but never duplicate it, no two paintings of course being the same. So it was that Jakob Goldschmidt attempted to recover his collection as well. He was not the only victim of Nazism to seek restitution after the war, but he was one of the most visible. He worked through the State Department, through various Jewish restitution organizations, and through a young New York lawyer who had made art restitution a specialty. Jesse Wolff, a partner in the then-small firm of Weil, Gotshal & Manges, was the lawyer.

Goldschmidt and Wolff spent endless hours on his collection. Some of it was traced to a 1942 Nazi auction of Jewish property, including one of the most important assemblies of art sold during the war. Other pieces were lost to the free trade— in artworks and jewels, possession equals title. In both cases title would be a problem for those seeking restitution. Unlike real estate, or even automobiles and boats, artworks rarely change hands with legally binding titles. It was one thing to claim you had owned, say, a Cézanne landscape. It was another to prove you had. Even against these odds, Goldschmidt and Wolff managed to recover a few of his pictures.

For Wolff, restitution of stolen Jewish property was not merely a way to bring new business into the firm. It was a personal obsession that would never leave him, a way, perhaps, of venting his anger over the inhumanity of the Holocaust. A brahmin New York Jew, Wolff, with his quiet and impeccable manners, dark hair, and olive skin, could pass for an Egyptian or Persian prince. His wife, Betty, is the sister of the late well-known art critic Tom Hess. An art lover and a loner who sails for relaxation, Wolff can be found dining solo in the cafeteria of the General Motors Building, where his office is in New York. From the time of the Goldschmidt sale, Wolff came to represent Sotheby's in American legal matters and sit on its board of directors—but not because the negotiations with the Goldschmidt heirs went so smoothly.

The odd thing about Goldschmidt's zeal to reclaim his lost artworks is this: He did not intend to leave them to his children. He was the type of collector whose passion for art ran deep. His children and widow did not, at least in his eyes, share this passion. He saw little reason to leave them pictures they could not fully appreciate. Fellow collectors should have the opportunity to enjoy the Cézannes and Van Goghs and Renoirs he had gathered together. This was the main reason collectors like Goldschmidt caught Wilson's eye.

"In Europe," Wilson explained, "and of course in Great Britain, families do not sell their property, including their artworks, until they are destitute. It passes from generation to generation. In America, one generation forms a collection; the next generation forms another collection. On and on it goes, buying and selling, buying and selling. What could be more attractive to an auctioneer?"

The problem was that business is conducted differently in America than it is in Britain, a difference Wilson was willing to overlook, with the aid of Wolff.

Tough is a word often used to describe the elder Goldschmidt, who could discuss the fine points of Cézanne with the skill of a seasoned scholar. But as tough as the man was, his children were even tougher. From the time of Jakob's death in 1955 to Sotheby's final auction three years later, Erwin Goldschmidt would set auction records of a sort of his own. He would refuse to sign the contract Sotheby's requires of all consignors. He would threaten to sue his lawyer in public places where others could overhear this embarrassing indiscretion. In the eleventh hour, after invitations had been issued, catalogs printed, and media lined up for the big event, he would nearly sell the whole lot to a Greek shipping magnate.

What really made Wilson nervous was something else: Goldschmidt had forced Sotheby's hand on the negotiations. Instead of the standard 10 percent the firm then took from consignors, a brand-new and incredibly complicated system was agreed upon. Wilson is credited with having devised it. Although details remain fuzzy and many deny that it even existed, the system worked like this: Sotheby's guaranteed to Erwin Goldschmidt that his father's pictures would bring a set sum. If the pictures failed to reach that sum, Sotheby's would pay it to him anyway, out of pocket. Once a certain barrier had been broken, however, Sotheby's would receive much more than 10 percent of the proceeds. Sotheby's would either fly or fall—in front of the world.

Media from around the world had turned out for the sale. Even weeks before the October event much ink was devoted to the collecting Goldschmidts and their seven masterworks of French Impressionism and post-Impressionism. London was promoted as the center of the world art market. To lure the popular press, which was not usually concerned with art sales or artworks, Erwin Goldschmidt and his wife, Madge, were transformed into American success stories: his passion for collecting vintage cars, her style and relaxed (so American) manner. Even his hair was a subject of interest; the *Daily Mail* called it "crinkly."

The day of the sale Sotheby's held a dress rehearsal for the benefit of the broadcast media and to test the lighting and closed-circuit television equipment. Wilson auctioned off his associate, Carmen Gronau, for £42,000. "Poor Mrs. Gronau," he quipped as he dropped the hammer on the final mock bid in the flesh auction. Two hours before the 9:30 sale, the police were called in. A mob, gathering outside the New Bond Street salesroom, was trying to gatecrash the auction.

The arrival of the invited guests at 9:00 P.M. formed a new mob. More than half the invitations had been issued to Americans, and there was much clamoring and back-patting as the new moguls and art dealers held a Yankee reunion on the streets of Mayfair. It was a new type of art buyer and a new type of American—lusty, self-confident, eager to prove their position through their possessions, certain that the dollar was the currency of the future.

At precisely 9:30, the time the sale was scheduled to begin, there was no sign of Peter Wilson. No one really noticed at first. The din was so loud that several later compared it to that of a train station. Wilson was late because he was busy dealing with an unfortunate incident that nearly marred the whole evening. As Erwin and Madge Goldschmidt struggled to find their seats in the crowd, a man who had worked for Sotheby's promoting sales called out to a friend within earshot of the Goldschmidts.

"This is great," he said sarcastically. "We've got the room full of Jews!"

Goldschmidt flew into a rage. He stalked across the crowded room in search of Wilson and Sotheby's other key staffers. Wilson was about to mount the stairs to the pulpitlike rostrum at the front of the green-painted room. "Either that man is bodily removed from the salesroom or the sale is off," Goldschmidt told the auctioneer firmly. He pointed across the room to the culprit.

Fortunately the commotion in the room diverted all attention from these goings-on. Exercising awesome diplomacy, Wilson managed to persuade the man to leave without resorting to force. Goldschmidt was placated one more time. Wilson finally mounted the steps at 9:40.

"Chubby cheeked Wilson blinked in the glare of the massed T.V. lamps," the *Daily Mail* reported the next day, "ran his eye over the mink and diamond dappled audience, rather like a nervous preacher facing his first congregation, and rapped firmly on the ivory gavel. The sound, amplified by the microphones, stilled the chatter. Then to a great movement of anticipation and craning of necks, the first picture was carried in by two cerise colored [*sic*] attendants. It was Edouard Manet's self-portrait."

Once the sale was under way, Wilson's uneasiness vanished. Like the stage fright experienced by many great actors, for Wilson there would always be butterflies in his stomach the day of a big sale. Fortunately, for this, his first sale, Sotheby's had made record-keeping easier to follow. Reserve or minimum acceptable bids arranged between the consignor and auctioneer are normally written in code in the catalog used only by the auctioneer. This is because the reserve prices are deep secrets that, if known, could hurt the outcome of a sale, the reasoning being that prospective bidders would lower their sights in keeping with the reserve. For this sale the code was abandoned and reserves written out in plain English as an aid to Wilson, the neophyte.

But soon Wilson began visibly to relax and hit his stride, like a runner finishing his first mile ahead of schedule. The Manet self-portrait fetched $182,000 (£65,000), and the other three first lots brought more than their reserve prices as well. Normally the first three lots of a sale are the lowest-priced lots, the theory being that these are warm-ups for the bigger game. And indeed, $182,000 would be the lowest amount paid in tonight's sale of seven masterworks. In 1958 dollars, $182,000 would have bought a mansion and estate worth $3 or $4 million in 1985 dollars.

Manet's *"Rue Mosnier"* was the first picture to break the £100,000 (or $280,000) barrier, going for $316,400. According to the *Daily Express*, at £100,000, "the grey head of Somerset Maugham shook slowly in amazement. Dame Margot Fonteyn, in an off-the-shoulder eau-de-nil dress, stood on her famous toes craning with excitement. An iron-grey man dropped his monocle under foot." Wilson appeared nonplussed by the exorbitant prices. He was on a roll.

In 1980, Henry Ford II sold Vincent van Gogh's *"Jardin Public à Arles"* through Christie's in New York for $5.2 million. Tonight bidding for the same picture began at $56,000, and Wilson looked nervous again. "By this time," the *Mail* reported, "the uproar was rising higher than the temperature. Again the gavel rapped for order." Wilson was nervous because the reserve or minimum bid Goldschmidt would accept for the picture was $330,400. Bidding climbed slowly— painfully—to the $300,000 mark. For more than a minute there were no further bids despite Wilson's gentle pleas for more from the audience. Finally the bidding began again, and very slowly crept to the closing bid of $369,600.

Bidding for the final lot again started at $56,000. This was considered the star lot of the sale, a portrait of a young boy by Paul Cézanne, *"Garçon au Gilet Rouge."* The bidding became a contest, a fight to the end, between two New York dealers. Back and forth. Back and forth. The crowd was struck dumb. As nearly everyone sat glued to their seats, Wilson handled the battle like a croupier in a gambling casino, elegant, restrained, and uninvolved. Finally, when the bids stopped at $616,000, he leaned gracefully over the side of the podium and issued his famous admonition. "What," he said incredulously, "will no one offer more?" The crowd roared. The whole audience stood on their chairs and clapped and clapped. "It sounded," the *Mail* concluded, "like a Covent Garden great occasion."

Wilson was onto something big. Nothing like this had happened at Sotheby's before. A new game for the super-rich had been invented. It was called art-auction madness. All you needed to play were unlimited sums of money and an inclination to understand the fine points of fine art: a perfect marriage of the ridiculous and the sublime. What could be more attractive to the bored millionaires of the world? Greek shipping magnates and Swiss industrialists could play—and would, with gusto. But American millionaires play hardest. Like gambling, but more cerebral. Like horse racing, but cleaner. Art auctions became the sport of the late twentieth century, and Wilson led the way.

Rockefellers, Fords, Mellons, Goulds, Onassises, Niarchoses, Whitneys, Vanderbilts, Agnellis would all become major players, as would those who longed to be associated with the names of big money and social clout. For what better way to announce you had arrived than to drop a big bundle on a painting at an auction covered by the press and followed by international society? The rules of the game were ripe for exploitation, for there are no winners or losers in the art game—or so the party line goes. There are only believers. No matter what your nationality, religion, or ethnic extraction, you too can believe. Wilson would say that the price of art will only go up. But to true converts to the new international religion of art and beauty, price was the least of it.

Paul Mellon, scion of one of America's leading families and main backer of the National Gallery of Art, expressed the convert's belief neatly just after the Goldschmidt sale. The occasion was a lunch at the Metropolitan Club in Washington. Mellon asked his companion, a well-known art dealer, what he thought of "*Garçon au Gilet Rouge*," the Cézanne portrait of a boy in a red waistcoat. "Did I," he asked, "pay too much money for

it?" Now $660,000 was an awful lot of money to pay for any-
thing in 1958. But before the friend could answer Mellon truthfully, the scion answered his own question.

"You stand in front of a picture like that," he said rever-
ently, "and what is money?"

THREE

EVERYONE knows business meetings can be long and frustrating. The question is: What do you do about it?

For Peter Cecil Wilson the answer was obvious. Say you are negotiating for the purchase of America's leading art auction house. The year is 1964. The time is summer; the place, Parke-Bernet's offices on Madison Avenue and 76th Street in New York. Talks have dragged on for weeks. The main issue at hand is Parke-Bernet's lease for 980 Madison Avenue. The lease is the firm's main asset and you are not going to let disposition of the main asset remain undecided. It is hot, fetid in fact. This blasted American heat. You understand why British foreign service officers receive hazard pay for working in America.

What you do is simply take your papers and toss them into the air. Then, while the mimeographed documents float slowly downward like so many small white kites, you stand up and glare at the others, turn on your heel, and march out of the room. You don't have to slam the door behind you. You've already made your point. Further dramatics might seem excessive; they might think you a prima donna.

They know you mean business.

Few people know exactly what motivated Wilson, but nearly everyone could see that whatever it was, was powerful. By 1964 you could travel as fast as a jet plane, and Wilson was among the first in the group known as the jet set. But even jet travel frustrated him. Though he never complained of jet lag, he often complained about the time he spent in the air. One day he might be found in New York. The next he would be back in London. Two days later he would land in Tokyo for a whirlwind tour. The next week he would head for Johannesburg and Nairobi, only to land in Rome for a few days and wind up in his hideaway outside Grasse on the Côte d'Azur. The following week his schedule might be reversed.

For Wilson was a modern-day white hunter. His prey was works of art and antiquities, and more to the point, those who owned them. "Demand," he once explained, "is not the problem. The problem is supply." He probably would have made a good career intelligence officer. Up until the very end of his life he carried around a vast amount of knowledge about the very rich of the world: individuals, governments, and institutions. Precious few confidants were privy to the Wilson inventory.

"He would wake me up at six in the morning," one associate recalled, "to tell me that he had a hunch a Lady So-and-So could use some money. Now Lady So-and-So might be living in Palm Beach or Rome—I mean, the expatriate out-of-sight sort you would not normally think about. But he knew. And the frightening thing was that he knew exactly what she had in her collection, down to the last diamond clips."

The year after the Goldschmidt sale Wilson had already achieved his initial goal. He had been chairman of Sotheby's for only one year and the firm had already surpassed, nearly doubled, the sales posted by Christie's. Each year thereafter Sotheby's would top Christie's—and any other competitor—by nearly two times annual turnover. Small wonder that Wilson was frustrated. The challenge, it seems, had been taken away from him. He could have merged Sotheby's with Christie's. But then the challenge would really vanish; and anyway, the Mergers and Monopolies Commission of Great Britain would never allow such a merger. It would create a monopoly in the art market, one of the few prides of the otherwise moribund British business community.

The only challenge for Wilson was expanding Sotheby's market share around the world. So Wilson set up offices in Johannesburg and Cologne. He flew to Tokyo and introduced the entirely Western concept of auctions to the Japanese. He arranged the first sale of Russian works of art from the Kremlin to raise money for cash-hungry Soviets. Offices were opened in Sydney and Florence and New York. By the end of the seventies Sotheby's name would be known in fifty-six cities on six continents.

This was not necessarily the most efficient system. Holding sales out of the country was costly and at times tough to organize. In Japan, for instance, the first auction had to be re-called. The Japanese failed to grasp one essential point: Whoever holds his hand up buys the lot, and there was pandemonium afterward. In Holland the auction system worked in reverse. The auctioneer begins bidding with the highest possible price he can ask. In a system not unlike a game of chicken, the auctioneer lowers the figure slowly until someone has the courage to bid on the lot. Then the piece is sold to that bidder without further fanfare. The system works well in the Netherlands, but not elsewhere.

In Egypt, Sotheby's encountered cultural barriers of another stripe. Those present still shake their heads slowly when the 1954 marathon auction in Cairo is mentioned. For what should have been a major art-marketing event turned into the biggest fiasco in the history of the field. Negotiations began in 1952 between Sotheby's and the new Egyptian government under General Naguib and, later, Nasser. King Farouk, as you may remember, had already abdicated and fled into voluntary exile with barely the shirt on his back. Would Sotheby's sell the king's possessions, the new socialist government wanted to know?

The question would have whetted any art dealer's appetite, and Sotheby's was no exception. Among royal possessors, the king was near the top of the list. "The numbers and opulence (and sometimes vulgarity) of every type of luxury article made by master craftsmen from all countries and periods was simply mind-boggling," Frank Herrmann wrote in the authorized 1981 biography *Sotheby's: Portrait of an Auction House*, "the gold boxes often encrusted with jewels, the two thousand magnificent gold watches, the Swiss automata (moving boxes and figurines), the enamel pieces by Fabergé . . ."

Farouk's taste and mania for possessions crossed all barriers: "In parts of the palace [we] found an immense collection of early aspirin bottles, paper-clips and even razor blades. . . . Farouk had dispatched agents to find rare examples of such things in remote villages as far away as Persia and Argentina." Then there was another aspect to his collecting: his "far-reaching and well known collection of erotica and pornography, housed in some *twenty* rooms." Even before the contents were cataloged, the British Museum expressed an interest in the erotica and pornography.

The first Sotheby's agents tackled the palace and its contents in 1952. Two years later they were still there, but not without bruises. The revolutionary government was very unsure of itself and, according to one agent on hand in Cairo, "touchy to the point of distraction. The slightest adverse comment or clumsily constructed question tended to be interpreted with political overtones."

One of the first stumbling blocks was the legal rights of the dispossessed king. After much discussion with senior ministers, a bill was passed specifically to cover this point. Not only was the king dispossessed, but his entourage was cut out as well, including three ex-queens, some fifty-nine ex-princesses, and twenty-nine ex-princes, none of whom was prepared to accept the sale without protest. Then there was the matter of where the sale should be held. Sotheby's pushed for a sale in London, where the exposure and central location would bring the highest results. This was out of the question, as far as the Egyptians were concerned.

"The Palace Collections of Egypt" were sold by Sotheby's at Kubba Palace in Cairo in March 1954. The palace "looked its best for the occasion," Herrmann recalled. "Outside on the

neatly trimmed lawns and among the flower beds and banks of
blazing bougainvillea blossoms, guests strolled around discussing their purchases or pausing to sip cool drinks from glasses
tinkling with ice, served by courteous servants in the familiar
tarboosh and white galabia. A brass band played military
music and Viennese waltzes in the gardens throughout
the sales. . . .

"It was the end of an era."

British Overseas Airways Corporation linked London with
Cairo in a special charter flight for the sale. The garden party
atmosphere, so out of place in the new people's government of
Egypt, was put on primarily for the benefit of romantic Westerners. Unfortunately, Egyptians had little use for such mem-
ories of the all-too-recent past.

Egyptian buyers were almost completely absent from the
bidding. In the prevailing socialist climate, it probably seemed
unwise to be seen paying large sums of money for royal property. For Westerners, the sale provided a chance to pick up some
royal bargains from the vast array of detritus. Most of the razor blades went unsold by the end of the day and Sotheby's came
in several million dollars under the estimate for the sale. The
Egyptians refused to pay the imperialist auction house.

The Egyptian undersecretary of finance was placed under
house arrest, yet Sotheby's still could not collect its money. Then
the Suez Canal blockade began. The situation went from bad
to worse. Sotheby's had to drop its claim against Egypt for the
sake of a more important diplomatic issue: the reopening of the
canal. Until the 1976 OPEC oil shortage drove up prices and
London became second home for much of the wealth of oil-pro-
ducing nations, Sotheby's would not have much to do with the
Middle East.

Small wonder then that Wilson lived with one eye always
focused on the United States. America enjoyed unbridled prosperity under Eisenhower, the retired war hero with his taste
for genteel games of golf, nasturtium salads, and a wife who wore
haute couture dresses by Charles James. "Palm Beach," Wilson once recalled fondly. "I had never seen anything like it. All

I could think was: This is where the action is. Palm trees, warm winters, oranges, and lots of big houses begging to be furnished properly."

Wilson first laid eyes on Palm Beach during the winter of 1947. He was there because he had left MI-5 and returned to Sotheby's. Part of his new duties, as he saw it, was cultivating rich Americans. And where else could you find rich Americans but in Palm Beach, a fourteen-by-one-mile manicured sandbar on the southeast Florida coast where diamonds outnumber seashells. The tall and elegant auctioneer with impeccable manners was much in demand by leading Anglophile hostesses, who also entertained the Duke and Duchess of Windsor, the Duchess of Argyll, and other titled Britons short on cash in their tight postwar homeland but long on pedigree, which midwestern millionaires like the Charles Wrightsmans so avidly sought.

Wilson immediately saw that Sotheby's could do brisk business in America if only one problem could be solved: Transport to London ate up profits in many cases. He was looking for an American base for Sotheby's. And he found it in Parke-Bernet Galleries, the leading American art auction house, located on 57th Street in New York. But he had to wait awhile. Preliminary negotiations for a merger between the two houses ended when Wilson had to admit one sad fact of postwar Britain: The British Treasury would not permit export of pounds sterling to purchase an overseas business.

By the 1958–1959 season, imports of American property resuscitated the British auction rooms, none more than Sotheby's. By the beginning of 1960, Sotheby's boasted a New York office to handle the influx. Under the watchful eye of Wilson—and his Palm Beach connections—the New York office took in more things to sell across the Atlantic than Parke-Bernet did to sell in New York. Sotheby's, operating so brilliantly under the handicap of three thousand miles of travel, was clearly a threat to Parke-Bernet (or P.B., as the firm was known to the old families of New York and the Eastern Seaboard who had used its services for nearly a hundred years). In the lobby of P.B.'s new ultramodern sale space at 980 Madison Avenue, the sight of the elegant men from Sotheby's, boldly carrying catalogs blazoned with the competition's name, would send shivers through the place.

Sotheby's New York team was a lean but fierce rival. Jesse Wolff, who had smoothed the complex Goldschmidt sale and won Wilson's lifelong friendship, continued to handle the intricate legal end of Southeby's American operation, including difficult import/export licenses and litigious American consignors. At the helm of the New York operation was a young Englishman whom Wilson couldn't live with and couldn't live without. He was Peregrine Pollen, a sinewy Etonian who would probably have excelled in any business or service endeavor.

In London, Wilson had gathered a large team of talented—and in some cases not so talented—young men, all of whom were, if nothing else, immensely presentable. Wilson's Boys, as the young sixties-style mods in bell-bottom tailored suit pants and paisley-lined suit coats were known, became regular fixtures in both smart and swinging London circles. Many of them, like the author Bruce Chatwin and current head of Sotheby's paintings department David Nash, arrived at Sotheby's very young from humble backgrounds. Wilson became both father figure and father confessor, and the "boys" owed him varying degrees of allegiance.

Pollen was never one of Wilson's Boys. While still at Eton he distinguished himself with tests of endurance, rowing a mile, swimming a mile, and bicycling a mile in less than fifteen minutes altogether, a record that remained unbroken for some time. A born leader in the great British tradition of colonial governors, having served as aide-de-camp under Sir Evelyn Baring in Kenya, Pollen had more to offer Sotheby's than good looks or an eye for art. And in fact, he was not good-looking. Tall, long-waisted, and bony in a particularly Anglo-Saxon way, complete with aquiline nose and protruding ears, he was the perfect counterpart to Wilson's smooth good looks and Wolff's swarthy handsomeness. The three made a good team, at least from outward appearances.

Pollen took his duties in America seriously. Before long it became clear that his duties involved the acquisition of Parke-Bernet. He and Wilson pushed the issue through the London board, though not without some opposition. To the hidebound board members, operating in America would open a can of worms. Wilson and Pollen made a compelling presentation.

The division of duties in America followed a colonial format. Wilson took on most negotiations, traveling from London to New York via BOAC weekly. Pollen handled the details. Wolff handled the legal matters involved in a transatlantic merger, as the acquisition of Parke-Bernet was euphemistically called during the various meetings between the two parties. Little did they know that the deal would require two years of insufferable conference.

Nearly two hundred years after the Treaty of Paris ended warfare between Britain and America, the battle was rekindled at Parke-Bernet in 1964. Wilson, Pollen, and Wolff would arrive looking crisp, well tailored, and not a little officious and arrogant, according to one of the participants. Sotheby's was a world leader. Parke-Bernet was a provincial auction house— granted one that, as holder of the $2.3 million world record for Rembrandt's "Aristotle Contemplating the Bust of Homer," could not be ignored.

Leading the Parke-Bernet team was Leslie Hyam, the autocratic British-born president. Wilson and Hyam immediately repelled each other. It was as much a matter of style and presence as position. A Cambridge-educated Jew who had afterward used the Metropolitan Museum of Art as his classroom, Hyam felt strongly that Parke-Bernet should be run as it had been run under his leadership. A merger in parts, Wilson maintained at one of the legendary meetings that ended with his storming out and slamming the door, "was a two-headed dragon!"

Hyam once confessed to a friend that he had emigrated from England in the thirties to get away from people like Wilson. And here he was under the man's thumb, or so it seemed to him. Wilson did little to assuage Hyam and the other directors of Parke-Bernet, who included Louis Marion, a scrappy red-headed auctioneer whose son John would later head the New York office, and Ralph Colin, a prominent New York collector who had been one of the original partners in CBS and who represented Parke-Bernet's legal interests.

Then Hyam died.

The autopsy gave as reason for death a heart attack. His close friends—including Marion—felt he had committed suicide. The reason they gave was an acute depression Hyam had confessed to during the weeks before his death. The world he had created was slipping through his fingers, like sand through an hourglass. A failed love affair only added to his malaise, they said. Other than that it was felt that Hyam was in perfect health—an unlikely candidate for a heart attack.

With Hyam out of the picture, it would have seemed to the British that Parke-Bernet was theirs for the asking. This was not the case. Hyam's heirs, eager to settle his estate, had sold his share in Parke-Bernet to an acrimonious American called Colonel Richard Gimbel, a flag-waving patriot who kept his distaste for all things British no secret. Unlike Hyam, however, Gimbel was unable to rally Parke-Bernet's other directors and shareholders behind him. But there were further obstacles in the way.

Ralph Colin, whose nomination to the board of the Museum of Modern Art had been blocked due to undisclosed improprieties, was eager to retain his relationship with Parke-Bernet. He enjoyed the insider's track in the art market and the perks—social, financial, and otherwise—that it implied. He took two major steps to protect his investment in the auction house. Colin first appealed to the Justice Department to investigate the possibility that Sotheby's take-over would create a monopoly. After the Justice Department turned down his request, he appealed to Lord Harlech, who as David Ormsby Gore served as British ambassador to Washington during the Kennedy and Johnson administrations.

As British ambassador, however, Harlech had little real power. He could only look into the matter. And he did, with great gusto. At the time he was rumored as the leading candidate for the hand of the widowed First Lady Jacqueline Kennedy. Going to bat for Parke-Bernet, including trips to New York for meetings and so on, only added to his luster, or so he presumably thought. Harlech and Colin would not end their relationship here. In a matter of years, Pamela Colin, Ralph's daughter, would marry Harlech after a publicly orchestrated courtship. "She got what she wanted," the writer Gaia Servadio once said of the union, "and he got what he deserved." Afterward, Harlech would be known in private and in such satirical journals as *Private Eye* as the Lord For Hire.

By spring 1964, Colonel Gimbel, Colin, and Harlech had lost control of Parke-Bernet. The other shareholders had decided to accept Sotheby's offer and agree to what was still called a merger. The final skirmish occurred in the press. Colonel Gimbel, never willing to miss an opportunity for drama, gave full vent to his anger: "The American flag," he told the *New York Herald Tribune*, "has been sold down the river."

This only fueled further satire of the auction scene. "We have just returned from performing a stint of military duty, guarding the ramparts against all enemies of the republic, foreign and domestic," Earl G. Talbott wrote in the *Tribune*, "only to discover that in our absence the British had landed and made off with Parke-Bernet."

Wilson responded to Gimbel's remarks with characteristic finality. "I am sure you would find many people in my country," he said, eager to make a favorable comparison for himself, "who said the same thing when Ford bought into England." By comparing Ford in Britain and Sotheby's in the United States, Wilson had elevated himself to the ranks of big operators. But Wilson had won in America, and few Englishmen could make such a claim.

Within months rather than years it became clear that Sotheby's and Parke-Bernet had not merged, but that Sotheby's had subsumed its American cousin. The first sign was Louis Marion's resignation or, as he preferred, early retirement. Marion not only disliked Englishmen like Wilson and Pollen, he simply could not understand them. In his place he put his son John, who would one day be known as "America's favorite auctioneer." Young Marion would be an important link between Parke-Bernet and Sotheby's, although, like his father, he felt uncomfortable in too much British company. Wolff became Sotheby Parke Bernet's lawyer, eventually a director and key participant in the Anglo-American outfit. Pollen became the president of Parke-Bernet. Wilson, of course, ran the whole show and took most of the credit for any of the advances made (of which there would be countless over the next fifteen years).

The Pollen family had quite a stake in the merger. Although no one knew this at the time, Sotheby's did not have the cash on hand to buy Parke-Bernet. And it was Peregrine's wife, Annabella, who sort of arranged the loan for the purchase. Sotheby's had sent $200,000 toward the final figure of some $1.7 million, including a $100,000 bonus for senior executives. No further cash was promised; and since Parke-Bernet's shareholders wanted to be paid sooner than later, a loan had to be arranged for the rest. Annabella had a friend whose husband was a junior vice-president of Morgan Guaranty Trust, the tony millionaire's bank in New York.

She asked her friend to ask her husband if he would loan Sotheby's $1.5 million to buy Parke-Bernet. An appointment was set for the two husbands to meet. The arrangement would not seem nearly so oddly casual were there not more to the story of Sotheby's first loan in America. On the day of the appointment Pollen somehow wound up in the wrong office, with someone else's husband. After some embarrassing discussions in which the loan was flatly denied, the situation was finally straightened out.

Then there was the matter of the guarantee. Somehow signals had been crossed on this count too. Someone had to guarantee the loan in the event of a default, and none of Sotheby's directors was willing to do so. Banks were not nearly as lenient as they would become in the seventies. Morgan Guaranty wanted full repayment within three years, outrageous terms given Parke-Bernet's earning ability. London finally gave in to the power of Wilson's persuasion: A few of the directors along with one of the firm's major outside investors guaranteed the loan.

And within three years the loan was paid off. Wilson once again claimed a victory and consolidated his power on the board. Parke-Bernet under Pollen was run like Kenya or Ceylon under Queen Victoria, firmly and paternalistically. And if some of the Americans didn't like the way the situation excluded them, that was all right. There were always Englishmen willing to come

over for a few years and live in New York. And there was always a new crop of eager art-history students willing to learn
how the art market operates.

Sotheby Parke Bernet, as the new joint venture was called,
marched around the world to the drumbeat of ever-increasing
prices for works of art. Wilson could do no wrong in the years
to follow and the directors resisted his ideas less and less often.
Never mind that Wilson would constantly borrow more money
than the firm seemingly could repay. Britannia ruled the waves
once again, even if it was only "a load of old rubbish."

FOUR

I T was hard for anyone to imagine Sotheby's without Peter Wilson. The tall and elegant gentlemen, slightly stooped in a disarming manner, erudite and coolly dramatic behind the rostrum in front of a roomful of rich people, epitomized everything Sotheby's had become. Though international in scope —by 1979 the firm operated in fifty-six cities on six continents—it was small enough for one man to control every facet.

Suddenly, however, Sotheby's was without Peter Wilson. The news filtered privately through the upper management in September of 1979. "He called me at home," Pollen recalled somewhat poignantly. "I think he sounded upset about his decision. He said he would be retiring to France, sooner than later. Something about tax trouble and health. I think he gave those reasons in that order. Yes, it was a shock. I had always thought he would die in the rostrum. He just didn't seem like the type to retire."

On January 1, 1980, Wilson retired to Château de Clavary. He transferred his residence from Britain to France because, he said, he had to worry about death duties in Britain.

Sotheby's had made him a rich man and he wanted to leave his fortune intact to his two sons.

That Wilson loved his sons no one really doubted. His marriage may have ended long ago in divorce, but his two sons had such close ties to their father that one of them actually lived on the grounds at Château de Clavary. On the face of it, the explanation for his departure was sound. More than one Englishman had switched residences to avoid the steep taxation enforced on all British subjects. And if Wilson acted a little impulsively in this case, well, it was not the first time he had showed that side in public.

But those who knew him well found the explanation tough to swallow. Granted, he had come into a sizable new fortune since the 1977 public flotation of shares in Sotheby's. As one of the major shareholders, an investment of £200,000 sterling had mushroomed in a little over a year to several million pounds. But as one colleague bluntly put it: "*He* wouldn't be paying his death duties; his estate would. Wilson, I've told you before, would sell his own grandmother."

In private, speculation over his motives for emigrating ran wild. One of the main reasons for this was the timing of his sudden departure. By September 1979 nearly everyone in the inner circle in London knew that a major scandal was about to break. Andrew Boyle had written a book entitled *The Climate of Treason*, exposing, it was then thought, several members of the notorious and treasonous Burgess/Maclean/Philby spy ring. The spy ring was made up of effete sons of the decadent bourgeoisie who had been recruited as spies for Russia in the thirties and infiltrated the upper levels of MI-5 and MI-6 during the Second World War. Guy Burgess, Donald Maclean, and Kim Philby, all contemporaries of Wilson's and co-workers in Washington in MI-5 and MI-6, had defected to the Soviet Union long ago. Most believed this unfortunate chapter in British espionage had been closed for good—until now.

Wilson doubtless heard his name had been mentioned as one of the possible members of the spy ring. Having left his wife in 1948 to pursue open homosexual relationships, Wilson soon landed with a friend in Garden Lodge in Kensington. The friend was Thomas Harris, the art dealer who was also close to Guy Burgess, Donald Maclean, and Kim Philby. Wilson's connections with the triumvirate did not go unnoticed.

Only Wilson, the Kremlin, and Whitehall know the truth about Wilson's activities during and after MI-5. When asked point-blank about his activities in the secret service, Wilson was evasive and quick to explain that one did not "talk about such matters freely . . . the national security, you know . . ." When asked whether he was in fact a double agent for both the Soviets and British, he scoffed and said bluntly, "I wouldn't print that if I were you."

There was considerable talk in London in the fall of 1979 about Wilson's possible involvement. One couple who had served in MI-5 during and immediately following the war said they had always believed Wilson was a member of the spy ring. The couple, whom I will call Lord and Lady Mole, said they had even heard that Wilson continued to gather and sell information to whoever would pay the highest price, through his travels for Sotheby's. The couple is in a position to know such things, and put themselves at some risk by coming forward.

Lord and Lady Mole explained that Wilson could have used free trade and the privileged position of the art world for his dirty work. Art travels freely from country to country. Wilson traveled freely from country to country and in fact enjoyed access via Sotheby's to the upper levels of government and commerce in both the free and the communist world.

A colleague who worked closely with him recalls that Wilson seemed oddly uncomfortable about his early retirement. Even though he was sixty-six years old, he was a robust sixty-six-year-old who had never missed a day of work or talked about retirement as even a remote possibility. "I do recall him saying something very strange in retrospect. At the time I didn't think much of it. But now that it comes up again, I think it was strange. When he told me he was leaving, he said, 'I would never do anything to jeopardize the reputation of Sotheby's.' At the time I thought he meant that he would look after the company when he left. Now I see it could have had two meanings. He often did."

Wilson could have struck a deal with the government, much as others had done, in exchange for protection from embarrassing exposure. Sotheby's was, after all, one of the prides of the British commercial world. How would it look if the man running the firm was a Soviet spy? On November 21, 1979, live from BBC headquarters, Sir Anthony Blunt confessed that he had been a spy for the Soviets. As Surveyor of the King's Pictures and then Surveyor of the Queen's Pictures, Blunt had enjoyed a privileged position in the upper levels of the British royal family. He had been knighted Sir Anthony in 1956. In 1962 he had confessed secretly to his involvement in the Soviet spy ring, for which he was offered lifelong protection from public exposure. Unfortunately for him, Andrew Boyle discovered his identity while writing *The Climate of Treason* and forced Prime Minister Margaret Thatcher's hand. Thatcher could either suppress the book, a simple matter in cases of national security in the United Kingdom. Or she could expose Blunt as, in the words of the daily tabloids, THE MOLE IN THE PALACE. Queen Elizabeth II was forced to strip Blunt of his knighthood, the first time the royal family had done such a thing in more than fifty years. Blunt quit his position in the palace and retired to his West London flat, where he soon died, a broken man.

Blunt insisted that he had ended his contact with the Soviets in 1951. "I assumed [the past] would never come out," he said of his duplicity. Of his appointment, he said, "I simply thought here is a job in my own field, I think I can do it." There is no telling what Wilson thought when he heard his lifelong friend confess to his misdeed. Goronwy Rees, a former intelligence officer who had exposed Blunt privately in 1951, said that Blunt "lives up to your own sound definition of the classic agent as 'controlled schizophrenic' and who has so thoroughly mastered the art of lying that nothing will shake or break him down."

The same could have been said of Wilson. As a former spy, he loved intrigue and mystery. Even in casual conversations he seemed to be sending coded messages. He would skulk around Château de Clavary's ornate grounds talking to his secretary over a walkie-talkie, sometimes even emerging from the bush with the gadget in hand, antenna up.

Wilson moved deftly through the final months of 1979, carefully setting his succesors into place. With little fanfare, he departed for Château de Clavary, where he would die in a matter of years, a lonely man. There were no retirement dinners, no gold watches or speeches, no service pins after forty-three years with the company. "It was as though he didn't really leave at all," recalls one of his closer colleagues. "It was like, now you see him, now you don't. Most of us refused to admit to ourselves that he had actually left the firm."

Accordingly, there was very little fanfare in public over his resignation. The whole thing was dealt with as though it had been in the works all along. Sotheby's, if nothing else, knows how to manipulate the press, and the sudden resignation of Wilson was treated routinely. His choice of a successor made it clear that he intended to run the firm from his sunny tax exile. Lord Westmorland, Wilson's second cousin and close friend and confidant, would assume his place.

A logical successor would have been Peregrine Pollen or even the American Edward Lee Cave, both of whom had been groomed for the job. At least five other upper executives had hoped to be named. The irony is that Westmorland did *not* want to take over the reins at Sotheby's. "I told Peter that he should appoint a younger man who wants the job," Westmorland admitted candidly some years later. "I didn't want to run a big company. I am a director of a number of companies and can give good advice and make connections. But I am not an executive. I am not an art expert. And I know precious little about high finance. Peter finally convinced me to go ahead with the scheme. He told me he would be by my side whenever the need arose. That seemed like a proposition I could accept."

For all his limitations, at least Westmorland knows who he is. He is a member of the royal household. He is an accomplished horseman. He knows a great many people in the upper reaches of international society. And he does all this well, very well. He looks the part: tall, statuesque, with smooth German/English good looks complemented by rumpled but expensively tailored suits in dark shades of gray and blue, decorations pinned proudly to his sash on the proper occasions.

On first meeting, Westmorland appears warm and intimate, organized and duty-bound. He speaks slowly and carefully, in perfect English sentences and one of the most beautifully
punctuated accents in the language. In spite of his almost mili-
tary-style posture, he relaxes easily without unseemly show. The
fifteenth earl of Westmorland can cross his legs and pull up his
trouser without showing skin.

For Westmorland, Sotheby's was only one part of his identity, unlike Wilson and Pollen and many of the other directors
who wrapped themselves in the firm. There are some who say
he is overbred, like a springer spaniel, and of the fifteenth holder
of a title, that observation is easy to make. The unkind call him
Westie, like the breed of dog, behind his back. But Westmorland by all appearances is honest and forthright. He took over
the firm like a magistrate, signed the documents put before him,
asked very few questions of his subordinates, and if some of
them seem frightened of him, it is only because he does not seem
the type who can be easily reasoned with. For Westmorland,
there is a right way and a wrong way to do things. There is no
compromise.

At first no one noticed the change. The 1980–1981 season
reaped over $500 million in sales, nearly double the 1970–1971
season and a record in art market annals that would not be
matched for some time. Sotheby's was still the uncontested leader
in its field, the pride of the sinking empire, run by one of Her
Majesty's most loyal subjects. Wilson kept his word as well. For
the first year he guided the firm from his study off his Picasso
mosaic-tiled foyer in Château de Clavary. "Every question, big
or small, needed an answer from Wilson. We had no one else
to turn to. The long-distance lines between London and Grasse
must have been jammed with the most confidential Sotheby's
information," one of the specialists recalled; and in fact, Wilson even tried unsuccessfully to buy a private phone hookup
between Clavary and Sotheby's.

There was no one else to turn to at Sotheby's for good reason. With Wilson's untimely departure and Westmorland's curious ascension, the firm was floundering. The most noticeable

loss was that of Pollen. "I don't know why Peregrine left in a huff," Wilson would later lament. "He just could not work well with other people. He was too temperamental. I don't know what he expected me to do—roll over?" That is exactly what Pollen expected Wilson would eventually do. And why shouldn't he? For nearly twenty years he had been groomed to take over. But from the time he returned from New York in 1972, his future with the firm was somewhat tenuous.

Pollen refuses to speak with any candor about his departure. But those who know him well say he was deeply wounded by Wilson and still bears a scar. He returned to London with his family, he told everyone, so his children could be educated in England, a common practice among English upper class. Once back in London, having brilliantly manged Parke-Bernet for eight years, he assumed he would be given an upper executive-level position, the right- or left-hand man to Wilson. What he found instead were a number of vaguely defined executive jobs having to do with overseas operations in North and South America, publicity, and—a very important function in the Anglo-American group—liaison between New York and London.

When Westmorland was given what Pollen thought should be his job, Pollen immediately expressed his displeasure. This may have been when Wilson decided that Pollen could not work well with others. A more vindictive sort would have done more damage than Pollen did; and in fact he would later act surprised to learn that his departure had been one of the key events in the decline and fall of Sotheby's. As it was, he left in a huff and sold off all his shares in Sotheby's. He should have given himself more credit. Pollen was one of the most dynamic leaders in Sotheby's, if not the most. A vacuum was formed by his absence that would not be filled for years.

But more important than his leadership abilities were his shares in Sotheby's stock. Pollen owned 900,000 shares of stock in a tightly held company, more than Wilson or any other director, more than almost anyone else. A sale of such a large block of stock would be bound to have an effect—and it did. Not to mention the fact that the market had already responded with characteristic fickleness to Wilson's departure. Worse yet, Wilson himself began quietly to sell off his shares, and other directors followed suit.

By 1982 you could pick up shares in Sotheby's for cheap. You could even buy out the whole lot if you really wanted to take on a risk. With only 17 percent of the stock where once 51 percent had been owned by directors, that left 83 percent floating freely. All you would need to declare yourself a victor in the stock market game known as take-over would be 50 percent plus 1, an investment of about $40 million.

This situation did not go unnoticed. Patrick Sergeant wrote that Sotheby's directors—particularly Wilson and Westmorland—had been aggressively promoting the company to outsiders. In his London *Evening Standard* column in January 1982, Sergeant speculated that Sotheby's itself was getting hammered down. Any interested parties picking up a tip from the Sergeant column, as many savvy businessmen often did, may have been dissuaded by another article. *Fortune*, the influential American magazine, painted a grim picture of Sotheby's. Under the heading SOTHEBY'S LOST ART: MANAGEMENT, *Fortune* told of bumbling incompetence coupled with egregious arrogance: In a word, *hubris* had come to haunt the hallowed halls of Sotheby's, as it had once plagued the Roman Empire.

Most of the blame for the firm's troubles was pinned on Wilson. In his absence, the article noted, the remaining executives had positioned themselves in warring camps. "Marcus Linell, the chief of experts, didn't get on with Graham Llewellyn or Peregrine Pollen; Llewellyn didn't get on with Pollen; Pollen didn't get on with Peter Spira, the group finance director; Spira didn't get on with Llewellyn: I've never seen anything like it." But while Sotheby's directors fought among themselves, like parentless children, the important American division was left to its own devices. And what devices!

Pollen and Wilson had been the major links between all the various divisions, which now wrapped around the world in fifty-six cities on six continents, and provided Sotheby's with as much income outside Britain as inside the United Kingdom. During the record-setting 1980–1981 season, the American branch—run from 980 Madison Avenue in New York and including salesrooms in Los Angeles and Palm Beach—accounted for more than half of the nearly $600 million in gross sales. Although many of the British directors were loath to admit it, without the U.S. operation Sotheby's would not have been Sotheby's; in fact, it would not even have been Christie's. Unfortunately, the British directors lost all control in the United States after Wilson and Pollen left.

John Marion, the affable son of Parke-Benet partner Louis Marion, was neither an art expert nor a financial genius, but rather a marketing man with a certain flair for theatrics and a down-home style behind the podium. "Come on, let's make it one hundred thousand," he once implored two bidders, much to the embarrassment of the statelier Englishmen, who felt he sounded like a carnival barker. "It'll sound better when you tell your friends about it." His knowledge of the art and antiques market, experts complained bitterly, was painfully inadequate, in spite of the fact that "he practically grew up in the place," as one pointed out incredulously. Many remember the time Sotheby's auctioned satellites, and "John thought that was the greatest thing we had ever done," the expert recalled, "because he knew what they were." The sale was a categorical flop.

Marion was a contrast to the other key directors in the United States, most of whom, like Wilson, were considered aesthetes. One of the main players was Robert Wooley, whose political abilities enabled him to be both Marion's and Wilson's confidant, no small feat considering that Marion and Wilson were normally at odds with each other. Wilson had discovered Wooley clerking in À La Vieille Russie, a midtown Manhattan shop that specializes in works of art from old Russia and boasts Malcolm Forbes, chairman of *Forbes* magazine, as its most regular customer. Following a lavish lunch meeting with Sotheby's executives, Wooley was hired in 1975 as an assistant cataloger in the decorative arts department. Rarely were catalogers taken to lunch anywhere. Wilson, it seemed, had plans other than clerking for Wooley.

Wooley was, on the face of it, an unlikely candidate for a

senior slot. Although, like Marion, he is charmingly down-to-earth, with a good sense of humor and winning style behind the podium, he is more presentable than handsome: medium height, prematurely balding, with a sartorial preference for loose American-style gray suits. Appearance in the world of Sotheby's, where matinee-idol good looks are preferable, counts for more than in most places.

Nor was he a sterling art historian. His expertise in the field of Russian works of art once backfired in public. The Smithsonian had called Sotheby's and asked for an appraisal of a silver object someone had donated to the Washington museum. Wooley gladly volunteered to assess the piece. The donor wanted to know how much he could deduct from his taxes for his tax-deductible gift to the nation, and of course he would want the highest possible appraisal. After several weeks of scrutiny, during which he could have called on other experts in universities or museums for a concurring opinion, Wooley confidently dated the piece and assessed its market value at somewhere around $100,000. The donor of course was delighted by his big deduction. A year later the scandal erupted. Wooley's silver piece was a fake, worth considerably less. The Smithsonian was embarrassed, but the donor was furious: The misattribution would cost him a lot of money in back taxes, not to mention accountant's fees and so on.

Even after the Smithsonian scandal, Wooley remained in charge of a major division of the firm. Politics may have had a lot to do with his immunity. Wooley frequently entertained Wilson overnight in New York in the style expected by the third son of Sir Matthew, fourth baronet. Some have said that a friend Wooley shared the apartment with footed the bill for the Fifth Avenue spread overlooking Central Park, complete with indoor aviary, although no one really knows for sure how the setup was maintained. Wooley learned quickly from Wilson how to utilize Sotheby's to his advantage, and in fact furnished his apartment with valuable pieces awaiting sale in Sotheby's warehouse. A porter who once moved furniture and artworks for Sotheby's recalled that Wooley maintained this unusual relationship with the firm: "His house was practically a second warehouse for Sotheby's. More than once, we would go over there and pick up things, chandeliers even, that he had decorating his apartment. They would be marked with a big Sotheby's tag when we got there." Others who were there for sumptuous dinners do not recall the furniture being tagged.

Edward Lee Cave, another Wilson protégé with considerably more experience, had a style that reminded older women of the Duke of Windsor or Cole Porter. Cave had launched the enormously successful Sotheby's International Realty division, which handles tony properties around the world, and worked very hard at his social connections, which were in fact very good after twenty years of dining out.

Cave and Wooley did not get along at all. In the absence of the mediating Wilson, their acrimony became open warfare. One day Wooley appeared in a neck brace, and a rumor spread quickly through the back bins of Sotheby's. Cave, the amusing story went, had broken Wooley's neck. Soon Cave would leave the firm, taking valuable clientele with him and setting up his own dealership nearby. Wilson was particularly upset over Cave's resignation, almost as upset, friends say, as he had been when the author Bruce Chatwin resigned some twenty years before. "I had hoped that Edward would take over the New York office," he said a few years later at Château de Clavary. "He had all the makings of a brilliant leader, but, alas."

There were, to be sure, other stars in Sotheby's American galaxy. David Nash, yet another Wilson protégé, had started in London at age fourteen, sweeping out the bins. He moved through the ranks to head the fine arts division in America by age thirty-four. But Nash had little interest in the politicking in the boardroom, and would soon abandon all but the most necessary management tasks. Another was William Stahl, Jr., the head of the American arts division, a well-turned-out blue-eyed boy who was once featured in a magazine spread on men with great style. Stahl was a protégé of Marion's, but after his marriage to society beauty Nancy Ireland, whom he met at Sotheby's, Stahl took a significant interest in riding with the hunt in exclusive

Millbrook, New York. James Lally, a quiet and brilliant scholar in Chinese art, went largely unnoticed because he lacked the charisma of Stahl or the aggressiveness of Wooley.

Almost by default, then, Wooley, had become the number two man at Sotheby's in New York, and there was little Westmorland could do, even if he had noticed any problem. And doubt had been cast upon Wooley not only by the Smithsonian caper but by other less publicized incidents. His expense account for the year 1981 exceeded all the other directors' expense accounts and many of their salaries as well. Some sources put the figure in excess of $50,000, although Wooley claims this is "poppycock."

Wooley was not the only big spender with company money; he was merely the most visible. The custom of mixing martinis with high finance has never caught on in London the way it has in New York for one good reason: There are no tax deductions for such frivolities in the U.K. Of course Sotheby's men in New York expected handsome allowances for lunches and dinners, not to mention countless other perks. And they got them, one way or another. After all, they have to entertain Collector DeVille in the Grosse Point style to which she is accustomed.

The head of the public relations department once beamed proudly that she ate both lunch and dinner five days a week at Les Pleiades, a fancy French restaurant around the corner from Sotheby's frequented by effete art dealers and blue-haired ladies. Lunch alone can set you back $100 for two.

Lunch was not the only thing that ate up Sotheby's profits. A woman who is now a successful New York art dealer recalls how her office was decorated when she was an assistant cataloger making $10,000 a year. There was a problem with lighting:

> We had no lights on our desks. The fluorescent fixtures were out or not yet installed—I've forgotten. Anyway, it was dark—windowless—and impossible to see. So we called downstairs [to maintenance] and told them about our problem. The next day they solved the problem. They sent up six or seven Tiffany lamps

scheduled for a sale in a couple of months. Now this
was during the great boom in prices for Tiffany lamps
[those colorful Art Nouveau lamps that became so
popular even McDonald's had copies made for their
hamburger outlets], and here we were making so little
money with $100,000 lamps on our desks. The irony
was delicious, if not a little bit unreal.

Anyway, I had mine on my desk for almost a year.
After a while I forgot what a valuable piece of property it was. I also forgot that the lamp actually belonged to someone else. I taped notes all over it, to the
edges of the beautiful stained-glass shade. I rested my
hats on top of it. One day I inadvertently knocked the
edge with, I think, my handbag. Well, a corner was
chipped off; part of the valuable glass inlay had come
undone. I told one of my co-workers about it and she
showed me what she did when accidents happened: She
took out a tube of Krazy Glue and reattached the
chipped piece. A few weeks later they recalled the lamp
for sale. No one knew about the damage and as far as
I know the lamp sold for a lot of money. I didn't follow the sale because I didn't want to draw any unnec-
essary attention to my little accident.

An estates and trust lawyer recalled an unfortunate run-in
his firm had with Sotheby's which was smoothed out by diplomatic John Marion. On the death of one of his clients, the lawyer immediately called Sotheby's, where he knew Marion through
mutual friends. Sotheby's agreed to dispose of the rich client's
personal effects and considerable collection of paintings and art
objects. Once the consignment had been moved to Sotheby's
warehouses and cataloged, the client's heirs began to notice that
"a few things were missing, among them a few very valuable
things." They complained to the lawyer, who in turn called
Marion and asked him what had happened to the missing things.

"The whole affair suddenly got out of hand," the lawyer
remembers. "The heirs held me responsible. I could have gotten into a lot of trouble over this, fiduciary responsibility and

so on. On the other hand, Sotheby's could have claimed that they never saw the things. There were no records or inventories and it was one man's word against another, a big mess. But John handled it brilliantly. I won't say it was as though it was a routine problem. But he spoke personally with the heirs, calmed them down a lot, and eventually some of the things were found at Sotheby's. I think they had been mislaid in the bins or something like that."

No one noticed such abuses when business was booming and the share price was climbing. Within a few years, Marion predicted, Sotheby's would need three times as much space. He based his calculations on the assumption that Sotheby's growth pattern would be like that of any other business, which of course it would not be because Sotheby's is like no other business. Marion and Wooley lobbied vigorously for a new building in New York to house an expanded decorative-arts showroom and salesroom. By the time Marion found a new building, Wilson had just departed and the board was in disarray. Several of the British directors could not recall even discussing the new building, although the expansion had been talked about for several years.

Without, it seems, even a nod of approval from London, the team of Marion and Wooley poured $13 million into an abandoned Kodak film-processing warehouse. The original plan called for producing income by building an apartment tower on top of the five-story block-long building at York Avenue and 72nd Street, several miles from the established carriage trade on Madison Avenue and 57th Street. Only after the lease had been signed did the directors discover that the apartment scheme was structurally unfeasible. "The building would have been crushed like a pancake by such a structure," recalls an architect who worked on the renovation. "Any engineer could have told them, but they didn't even bother to ask. It was pie-in-the-sky time over there."

The apartment tower was meant to lure rich people over to that part of town. Marion pointed out that when Parke-Bernet moved from 57th Street to upper Madison Avenue in 1949, the art and antiques trade followed. "They will follow us again," he said, failing of course to grasp one essential point. Madison and 76th Street is in the middle of one of the richest neighborhoods in the world, flanked on the east by Park Avenue and the west by Fifth Avenue. It made good business sense for art and antiques dealers to move closer to their rich clientele. It made no sense whatsoever for them to move to a neighborhood like 72nd and York, populated largely by middle-class middle-management types more likely to buy furniture at Sloane's and art reproductions via mail order from the back of *The New Yorker*. As of this writing in 1985, no antiques or art dealers have followed Sotheby's across town to York Avenue and 72nd Street.

For the most part, the directors in London had no idea of the difference in neighborhoods in New York; and in fact, Westmorland humorously recalled looking at a prospective site on Union Square in lower Manhattan, one of the worst drug-pushing areas in town. "They told us," he said, shaking his head, "that the neighborhood would come up. Well, how could *I* tell? As far as I could see, New York neighborhoods were always coming up and going down—many at the same time." Nor did Westmorland realize many other differences between London and New York business practices.

Even Wilson had no idea what was going on in the York Avenue construction, the project having been begun shortly after he departed. Although Wilson spoke to Westmorland several times every day from the South of France, he spoke less often with New York, and then mainly with Wooley. Later he would admit that he was disappointed with the "first class all the way" results in the rather bland, ultramodern salesroom, which looked more like a suburban department store than a branch of an English auction house with close ties to the crown.

It was decorated predominantly in beige, in all that the color implies—"a soft, wool fabric, formerly undyed and unbleached," according to the dictionary, and related in origin to the word *bombast:* "talk or writing that sounds grand or important but has little meaning; pompous language." There is little doubt that Sotheby's had no idea the color beige could impart so much deep-rooted meaning. But Sotheby's York Avenue salesroom was—and is—beige, all $13 million of it.

And if the directors—like Wilson—seemed disappointed by the expanse of undyed wool fabric decorating a squat warehouse in the wrong part of town, they hid their displeasure only in public. Board meetings were another matter. Wooley's seat on the board was soon removed from him. Marion blamed everyone else, and of course he retained his seat on the board, primarily by default. He was the sole link between New York and London since Wilson and Pollen had departed.

Sotheby's internal problems didn't take long to find their way onto the books. In 1982, for the first time since Wilson took control of Sotheby's, archrival Christie's nearly pushed ahead of the firm. No one knew what to do. Sotheby's sales had been nearly double those of Christie's only the year before and, more or less, since 1958. Suddenly the rug had been pulled out from under everyone's feet, and many people were already scrambling, like Cave and Pollen, for securer ground. There was more bad news: For the first time since the Second World War, Sotheby's would post a loss for the season as well. The worst, though, was yet to come.

PART II

THE
WORST SORT OF
AMERICANS

FIVE

F ROM the fifty-seventh floor of Citicorp, a view stretches
across midtown Manhattan once enjoyed only by birds and
low-flying airplanes. But Marshall Cogan and Stephen Swid,
seated cheek-by-jowl behind a twenty-five-foot partners' desk
in an office as long as a bowling alley, are not admiring the view
this day. The two self-made moguls have grown accustomed to
the panoramic sight of the northern New Jersey hunt country
to the west and the Statue of Liberty to the south, although the
view still takes breath away from most visitors.

Both men's eyes scan several video screens, which list stock
movements on the New York, London, and American ex-
changes as well as several lesser markets in Asia, Europe, and
South America. Cogan and Swid regularly follow the major
markets of the world, but it is the London market in which they
are particularly interested this July day in 1982. Since London
is five hours ahead of New York time, by nine in the morning
on the fifty-seventh floor of Citicorp, it is fairly easy to see how
things are shaping up across the Atlantic. Without missing a beat,
both men nod about the price of shares in one English-based
firm: Sotheby Parke Bernet, p.l.c. (private limited company),

cannot go much lower, they agree, having discussed the firm over the past six months. Swid places an order for 10,000 shares, a minuscule investment of roughly $30,000—minuscule that is, for partners whose combined wealth some have put as high as $1 billion. Buying into Sotheby's is just one of countless investments Cogan and Swid will make each day for the next year.

The reason Cogan and Swid are plugged into markets around the world has as much to do with the past as with the present. Both men began their climb to the top in the stock market, and both enjoy the rough and tumble of daily trading. For the past couple of years, however, they have invested primarily on their own accounts. Tending their own fortunes is now a full-time job because, in the late seventies, they cornered the moribund market around the world for felt. Because one of the essential components of the beaten fabric is petrochemical, the felt industry suffered during the OPEC price wars that so hurt the economies of the Western world, and Cogan and Swid picked up the pieces under the name General Felt Industries.

The felt industry means little more to most people than hats. But felt has wide-ranging industrial applications, inside the engines of jet planes and inside automobile hoods to muffle sound, just for starters, or as carpet underlay. Felt is used in every country around the world. And General Felt Industries, a privately held Delaware-registered corporation owned by Marshall Cogan and Stephen Swid, practically controls the market.

With their earnings from felt, Cogan and Swid don't have to lose sleep wondering whether their grandchildren will go to Harvard. They need other reasons for their daily fix on the video hookup to the markets of the world. And they have them. What good is a fortune in felt when most people think of the soft and springy cloth as kid's stuff, manufactured by pounding and beating hair, fur, and fibers?

What good is cash without cachet?

So the two moguls entered phase two of moguldom. Rockefellers have done it; Astors and Vanderbilts too. After all, who cares any longer from what grubby products their fortunes sprang? Phase two for Cogan and Swid involved aggressively pursuing their interests in design and art. In the late seventies,

GFI—as General Felt Industries is called—purchased Knoll International, the leading manufacturer of fine furniture designed by such twentieth-century masters as Mies Van Der Rohe and Marcel Breuer. Not that Knoll wanted to be owned by GFI. Fortunately for Cogan and Swid, it had little choice in the matter. The world leader in architect-designed furniture had fallen on hard times, and the closely held WASP firm had to raise cash to keep going—cash GFI was willing to put up when no one else could be found. After a few good years, however, everyone was willing to let bygones be bygones, and the Knoll staff would tell anyone who asked that they were very happy indeed with their new owners.

They were accustomed to rebuffs and battles, these two savvy traders from middle-class Jewish America. Street-smart, as only those who have lifted themselves up by their bootstraps can be, Cogan and Swid expected no favors. Not that they were hotshot arbitrageurs or take-over masters or even particularly rough operators. That wasn't really their style. But they knew enough about the world of blue-chip coupons to know that money alone was not always enough.

With Knoll in their pocket, Cogan gained admission to the prestigious Architecture and Design Committee at the Museum of Modern Art, Nelson Rockefeller's museum; Swid was admitted to the board of the Guggenheim Museum, Peggy Guggenheim's museum. Houses in Southampton and apartments on Park Avenue followed. Some would still call them outsiders, but others might begin to fancy them as mavericks.

For Cogan, the driving force behind the duo, the maverick role must be congenial. He has a small and wiry frame and his thin, nasal voice is imprinted with an industrial Boston accent that probably made life tough for him at Harvard. But he wouldn't dream of changing the way he speaks, and even his secretary answers the phone like Lily Tomlin imitating a Brooklyn operator. The maverick pose allows him to enter Sotheby's salesroom dressed in a cardigan sweater and polo-style cotton jersey, sleeves pushed up to the elbows.

As a scholarship student at Harvard in the late fifties, Cogan, now forty-eight, developed liberal political sympathies that include lifelong admiration and support for Senator Edward Kennedy, his main Washington connection. Early on, Cogan educated himself through art classes and frequent visits to museums. By the time he made his first million he had already formed a sizable collection of contemporary and Impressionist artworks, with the help of his wife, Maureen.

Cogan suffered his first setback at the hands of Sanford Weill, who was for some time American Express's number two man. As young brokers they formed a firm bearing their names: Cogan, Berlind, Weill & Levitt. Cogan claims he was the mastermind of a deal that in 1970 merged the brokerage house with Hayden Stone (subsequently Shearson Hayden Stone), which by 1978 led to a merger with Loeb Rhoades and eventually with American Express. Unfortunately, Weill emerged the victor in the deal, although Cogan made a small bundle of cash. Cogan weathered this as best he could, but the deal stuck in his craw. He had in fact contributed to his own demise. In 1970 the Securities and Exchange Commission accused him of mismanaging a client's discretionary fund. Rather than face costly and further damaging litigation, he accepted a ban on trading, voluntarily and without any admission of guilt on his part. It was then that he teamed up with Stephen Swid, a licensed broker who had never been censured by the SEC.

That the unkind refer to the duo as the Wall Streeters' Simon & Garfunkel has to do with both their respective styles and their appearance. As Cogan—the Paul Simon of the two, both in appearance and contribution—once put it disarmingly: Swid's "the good-looking one."

Tall, sandy/gray-haired, sinewy, and graceful, Swid, even at forty-three, can still play a good game of basketball, as he did on scholarship at Ohio State University in the fifties. Unlike Cogan, whose business style tends toward a cerebral approach that makes him seem enigmatic and evasive, Swid is direct and confrontational. He can insist that a potential adversary sit directly across the table from him, "so we can see each other's eyes."

The son of Russian Jews who immigrated to the Bronx before New York City's poorest borough was predominantly Hispanic and Black, Swid is not only direct, he is blunt like a New York and canny. Whereas Cogan may have been handicapped by growing up in the shadow of Brahmin Boston, Swid's Bronx background might have led him to believe he could do anything he wanted to in life without worrying about what others would say. Growing up in mercantile New York, where the bottom line is the bottom line, sometimes has its rewards.

Swid is an extrovert—provocative, engaging, often using his hands to orchestrate what he says, as those with heavy New York accents often do. Cogan is the introvert—quiet, cautious, using his hands only to remind a listener to pay attention to him, by tapping on his arm or pulling at his sleeve. There is a rare symbiosis between the two, dressed almost identically in English tailored suits, like some of the more flamboyant British film moguls or record producers one sees at Tramps in London.

The first GFI/Knoll investment in Sotheby's went largely unnoticed. Not that it should have, but it did. Shares in Sotheby's had continued to nosedive well into 1982, despite gallant efforts to pull the place together. Any investment, particularly a large one, would have sent the price up, at least momentarily, and should have alerted someone that something was afoot. The price did in fact go up, but the hubristic directors probably thought that the firm had recovered its value after the drastic cost-saving campaign put into place earlier in the year.

Lord Westmorland had practically given up on Sotheby's by the beginning of 1982. He had insisted from the outset that his chairmanship be temporary, and after two years in the saddle he was itching to return to a more courtly life. Westmorland, however, is an honorable man. And honorable men do not abandon a sinking ship. What they do is find a logical and fitting successor. Everyone's conception of how a chairman should look and behave is different. For a traditionalist like Westmorland, who goes by the book, a chairman should have gray hair and more years behind him than in front of him —someone like himself or Wilson. There were very few at Sotheby's who met his specifications. So it was that Graham Llewellyn, the affable Welshman who headed the firm's jewelry division and some international operations, became the new chairman of Sotheby's in 1982. Llewellyn, at sixty, had few hairs remaining on his oval-shaped head, all of them gray.

There were times when it was difficult for some to distinguish between Wilson, Westmorland, and Llewellyn—at least at first blush. Not only were the threesome roughly the same height, build, and coloring—tall, broad, and fair—but they even dressed more or less the same, tending sartorially toward dark-blue conservatively cut Savile Row suits and dark four-in-hand ties. Llewellyn's aristocratic appearance was his own best invention, clearly modeled on the example provided every day by Wilson.

According to company lore Llewellyn arrived in London at age fifteen from the coal fields of dimmest Wales with an accent so thick that no one, save a fellow Welshman, could understand what he had to say. If England valued Horatio Alger stories as much as America does, Llewellyn would be the perfect example of rags-to-riches. He moved quickly through the ranks at Harrod's, one of London's smart department stores, before arriving at Sotheby's as specialist in the jewelry department. There, under Wilson's careful tutelage, Llewellyn developed the confidence and sycophantic charm found among tony shopkeepers all over London.

Westmorland and Wilson liked Llewellyn because he ingratiated himself with them, although neither man deluded himself into thinking Llewellyn was the leader they were looking for; rather, he was the figurehead they were looking for. Westmorland is also a thorough man, and like most thorough men, he realized he could not step down without leaving Sotheby's in the best shape he could. There was no way that he could leave the overall operation to Llewellyn, a man who giggled when nervous, badgered his subordinates far too often, and lacked the oversight to run a multinational like Sotheby's. Sotheby's needed more than a new chairman. Sotheby's needed, as Westmorland put it neatly, "a tonic . . . a shot in the arm."

So it was that Westmorland telephoned Gordon Brunton early in 1982. As president of the International Thomson Organisation, a billion-dollar-a-year communications and petrochemical conglomerate, Brunton had successfully, at least in

Westmorland's estimation, handled the sale of *The Times* of London to Rupert Murdoch, the Australian publishing magnate. Perhaps Brunton could also fix things at Sotheby's.

"Would you give us a hand with Sotheby's?" Westmorland asked Brunton. As one of the directors of Sotheby's, and Sotheby's merchant bank, Warburg, Brunton knew that the place was in a mess. He also knew the name *Sotheby's* had a certain allure to Lord Thomson, his employer and the chairman of International Thomson. Thomson, the son of a self-made man who was awarded his title after he made his fortune, had also entered phase two of moguldom, like Cogan and Swid. Added to the business publications and prosaic oil and mining operations that lined the Thomson coffer was at one time the prestigious *Times*, as well as *Burlington Antiques* magazine. Thomson had actually entered phase three; for having inherited a title and earned a place in the upper reaches of English aristocracy, he had begun to sell off the money-sucking parts of his publishing empire, like *The Times*.

Brunton had done most of the dirty work involved in sales and cutbacks in The Thomson Organisation. A stocky and contentious Canadian whose pronounced overbite and clipped speech only add to his ferociousness, Brunton is maniacally obsessed with details and "getting the job done *right*." He says he "knows how to work well with creative people," although the creative people he has worked with often do not respond warmly to the mention of his name.

"I have given some thought to your offer," he told Westmorland a few days later from his expansive office in West London. "And I am willing to give you a hand, under one condition: After I have sized up the problems at Sotheby's, whatever I say goes, without question. I must have total control. I will not ask you for a salary or bonuses or any other remuneration. I will get this thing back on the tracks and I will do it speedily."

Without so much as a vote from the board of directors, Gordon Brunton became the new non-executive chairman of Sotheby's to Llewellyn's executive chairmanship. Brunton would run the firm from his office in International Thomson; Llewellyn would appear to run Sotheby's from *his* office on New Bond

Street. Westmorland returned to the Queen's horse. Poor Peter Wilson was suddenly stripped of all his power and many of
his allies in the firm, having watched as Cave, Pollen, and
countless others departed for safer ground. Sotheby's was now
under a sort of state of siege, being run by the bank and by
outsiders.

"We had no idea what [Brunton] had in mind," Wooley
later lamented from his corner office on York Avenue. "After
all, he had offered to work for us free of charge. How could we
turn down such a generous offer? Was he pushing for a knighthood? Hah hah. That's a good one. I don't know—maybe he
was. That's an explanation I have heard but I don't know how
it works [over there]." Wooley would be one of Brunton's first
victims, having to give up his seat on the board of directors of
the group.

Brunton had no idea how tough his new volunteer work
would be. Within weeks rather than months he had noticed that
Sotheby's was caught in a dangerous "disinflationary trap," as
he put it, and needed "drastic measures to breathe new life into
the firm." Amid much speculation that the place was in fact
up for sale, Brunton did everything in his power to "restore
profitability," and he did so without taking into account the
fragile nature of the art market and Sotheby's dominant place
in it. How could he have known, this specialist in the creative
business, whose office boasted two paintings, of a nineteenth-
century ship and horse, and whose bookshelves contained only
trade publications? Sotheby's to him represented an old British
business that had once been the world leader in its field, home
of the record price for works of art, and "the price of art
will only go up." How could he have known that his actions would
touch off heated debate over the future of the market
itself?

After a methodical analysis of the figures and the executives still left at the firm, he discovered that surgery was the
only route open—spare the limbs and save the life. By June of
1982 he made his recommendations, and they were accepted
without question, though there was some grumbling behind his
back. John Marion recalls that most of the meetings consisted

of Brunton speaking at length about what was wrong with each
of them. "He didn't really seem to listen. He thought he had all
the answers."

SOTHEBY'S TO CLOSE IN NEW YORK AND L.A. ran the banner
headlines in papers around the world. Brunton had decided
to shut down the Madison Avenue salesroom built for Parke-
Bernet in 1949 and the Beverly Boulevard salesroom next door
to CBS Television headquarters in Los Angeles. The bad news
was compounded by other bad news from London: Sotheby's
would also lay off some five hundred employees, across the board
but primarily in the United States, where overhead had reached
an unsafe level.

"I had no choice," Brunton later said.

"I wouldn't have done things that way," Wilson, at Château de Clavary, later said. "The U.S. operation, well, that was
the future of the firm, the future I had built up slowly over the
years. In one fell swoop we found ourselves back in time. Yes,
I know the Los Angeles salesroom showed a profit for that year,
but L.A. seems so far from London and in many ways unnec-
essary. I suppose that was what he thought. I don't know. The
only thing I objected to was the finality of his decision. It could
have been better timed, or more discreetly done."

By the fall of 1982, *The New York Times* would run a front-
page story on the demise of the market for works of art and
antiques, based on Sotheby's drastic cutbacks. Granted, the story
would soon be retracted with a full and stately *mea culpa* from
the paper of record. The problem, it seems, was not the market
for works of art; it was *Sotheby's* market for works of art. The
worst blow was the loss of the Madison Avenue salesroom. Once
the center of a thriving arts and antiques marketplace, the
Madison Avenue salesroom, once shut, became a haunting re-
minder that Sotheby's had pulled away from the field, or as one
of the constantly disenchanted dealers put it: "left us high and
dry. You don't set yourself up as the barometer of the health
of the market and then pull out like that. It hurt all of us, but
most of all I suspect it hurt Sotheby's for a long time."

Brunton's cutbacks in America were about the most drastic anywhere. In London one of Sotheby's smaller salesrooms

was abandoned, and fewer than a hundred employees were laid off. This only widened the Anglo-American rift that had become a dominant feature in the decline and fall. The news that Brunton had ordered a new office in Australia at the same time he cut back in L.A. and New York further fueled the animosity. Not to mention the cuts he had made in the board of directors; whereas once the board had been comprised of a nearly equal number of Americans and British, under Brunton the number of Americans was whittled down to two essential representatives: the lawyer Jesse Wolff and America's favorite auctioneer, John Marion.

Wolff had been elevated to deputy non-executive chairman, directly under Brunton, usurping John Marion's position as head of the U.S. operations, although no one dared put it that way. From the ranks of some twenty-five executives, Brunton had found two useful allies: Julian Thompson, a world-ranking scholar in Chinese antiquities, a quiet and deliberate man; and Thompson's protégé, James Lally, a redheaded expert with an M.B.A. from Columbia and a Boston Irish accent he did much to disguise with Britishisms. Brunton found qualities in Thompson and Lally that few others possessed at Sotheby's: Both could read a balance sheet and discuss with ease what was on it; both could follow instructions with considerable cool and effectiveness. That neither man was a leader did not really bother Brunton. After all, he was the leader of the new Sotheby's under state of siege. "It was a one-man look at the whole operation," he said.

Brunton must have found the more flamboyant characters at Sotheby's rather frustrating. As a self-made man and a strong believer in Margaret Thatcher's Iron Maiden regime, he had little use for fluff. But fluff is Sotheby's stock in trade, and without some show of superciliousness or frippery, the firm loses much of its allure. Within weeks it became clear that Wooley, Stahl, Cave, even Marion, were distinctly out of favor in the new regime. Wilson of course had been stripped of nearly all his power. "The money men had a bigger say in things," he later said, somewhat philosophically. "They had to, then."

Marshall Cogan and Stephen Swid had never met Gordon

Brunton. Nor had they met John Marion or Peter Wilson or Julian Thompson or Graham Llewellyn or any of the Sotheby's cast of characters. Their interest in the firm was not in the people running it. Quite the contrary. From the beginning of their investment in Sotheby's, they felt that the upper management of the firm was a poor lot of misguided souls. What interested them about Sotheby's was the name and the service it provided. As both art collectors and finance men involved in world markets, they could see how Sotheby's could be run at a handsome profit. They felt they had a contribution to make, alongside the working experts.

In the beginning, they would later tell people, they had no interest in taking over Sotheby's. But that's what they all say. They say it was not until they were challenged publicly to a duel that they considered fighting to the finish. There may be some truth in Cogan and Swid's claim that they had no interest in owning Sotheby's in the beginning. For they made no effort to get to know the executives of the firm. And in fact, the first disclosure to Sotheby's of their interest came through a friend of a friend, a mutual friend of theirs and Jesse Wolff's.

"Who do you represent?" Wolff blared into the telephone. He was sitting behind his desk at Weil Gotshal, overlooking the Plaza Hotel, Central Park stretching nearly to the horizon. "I can't give you an answer unless you tell me who you represent. How can you call me and say you represent a client interested in *helping* Sotheby's and expect me to say yes to their offer unless you tell me who they are?

"I see, oh, I see," Wolff said, puffing on his pipe and wrinkling his brow. He glanced out the window and back to the cluttered desk in front of him. Sotheby's had been Wolff's home away from home for more than twenty-five years. He liked the place, and he wanted to make sure that its future was secure. The names Cogan and Swid and General Felt Industries meant little to him, but he knew they were not for Sotheby's. Cogan and Swid were part of a new army of rough-and-tumble traders whose Wall Street exploits had become legendary by the early 1980s. Part of their successes had come from very hostile takeovers that inflicted wounds and stripped people of their dig-

nity. Wolff, the patrician and old-style Jewish gentleman, felt
his hackles rise. One suspects he did not like the way they had
used someone else to approach him. And who would like being
used as a conduit into the ranks of the otherwise Gentile Sotheby's world?

"I don't think we have any need for their help, but I will
get back to you," Wolff sighed to his friend.

Now this, he must have thought.

SIX

THE meeting began oddly.

Cogan and Swid arrived promptly at the world head-quarters of the International Thomson Organisation at 11:00 A.M. on December 22, 1982. London is particularly alluring at Christmastime; and the two American Anglophiles, having snared a piece of the empire called Sotheby's, were particularly happy before their first meeting with the board of directors, even though the directors had already expressed deep misgivings about a union. Arrived at via Concorde from across the Atlantic, England was a storybook place, where a deferential driver in a sleek black Bentley ferried you to a sky-high suite of rooms in the modern Park Lane Hotel overlooking Hyde Park and Buckingham Palace on the edge of Mayfair.

With Christmas only three days away, the front of the big white door of the Thomson home office was decked with a pine bough, a long red ribbon trailing the greenery. Inside the five-story Georgian building, however, the oddness began. A brisk receptionist in a dark-blue pleated skirt and matching pullover firmly guided the two Americans into a darkened boardroom off the main lobby.

Then Brunton arrived, all smiles and pleasantries, without the other members of the board, to tell them they were in the wrong room, as though the mistake were theirs. He guided them through the hallways and upstairs to another room where they were told to wait. Bemused, the two Americans took in the surroundings of the Thomson home office. They noticed that the offices, like many in London, looked more like the Alumni House at Princeton than a billion-dollar enterprise, with Chippendale reproduction desks, wing chairs in leather, and paintings of ships and horses on the wood-paneled walls. After about five minutes another receptionist, similarly attired to the first and equally officious, arrived to lead them back to the first-floor boardroom where they had originally been placed. "Mr. Brunton will see you now," she said with finality, as though he had not yet seen them.

Cogan and Swid looked at each other and practically burst into laughter. As careful observers of business protocol, who both thought Henry Kissinger had a strange way of orchestrating business meetings, they had never encountered anything like this. The Kissinger style involved as much pomp and circumstance as one might expect from the self-styled grandee. Cogan and Swid, on first meeting with the former Secretary of State, had entered a long boardroom through double doors. At the opposite end of the room stood Kissinger, who waited patiently while the partners slowly made their way across the room to where he was standing. He then thrust out his hand and, according to Swid, "pulled me so close I could smell what he had eaten for lunch. He was telling us that he is important but also intimate."

Sotheby's was another matter. Brunton would later claim that the meeting was "all very civilized, you know"; and in fact, his first question to the duo was about tea, and how they would like theirs. One look around the faces in the boardroom, however, and the two Americans realized this was no tea party. Their suits suddenly felt tight and strange. A glare can penetrate deeper than any words, and glares were hurtling at them in quadraphonic.

After formalities and tea, Brunton's first words were harsh

and threatening. Red-faced with rage, he unleashed his fury on the partners. There are strong echoes in Brunton's diatribes of Margaret Thatcher telling Neil Kinnock that he is "totally and absolutely wrong!"

"YOU HAVE MADE A MISTAKE," Brunton told Cogan and Swid straightaway, enunciating each word with long pauses in between for emphasis. The mistake Cogan and Swid had made was not only buying into Sotheby's, but apparently pressing the directors for a meeting as well. The reason Brunton felt so strongly about this soon became clear: "You manufacture carpet underlay," he said, grimacing as he formed the words *manufacture* and *underlay*. "We auction works of fine art," he said proudly, establishing, at least in his mind, a class difference.

Were it not for Brunton's vituperative delivery, Cogan and Swid would have laughed at the whole thing, particularly the way Brunton closed his opening remarks. In a tone generally reserved for recalcitrant children by stuffy headmasters, he told them, "I want you to promise me one thing: that you will buy no more of Sotheby's stock, that you will leave us alone and go about your business elsewhere." Brunton truly believed that this was all he had to do to avert a take-over. When he was later asked why he disliked Cogan and Swid, he said, without a trace of irony, "Well, they did not listen to me. I told them not to buy more stock—and they did anyway."

Cogan and Swid had been buying up stock in Sotheby's with a vengeance. By December 14, 1982, the week before the odd meeting on Stratford Place, the two Americans surfaced as the largest single shareholders in the troubled auction house, by a long shot. Not that it was difficult or even expensive to pick up a few million shares in Sotheby's. In spite of Brunton's cutbacks and alleged restoration of profitability, the per-share price had remained incredibly depressed, as low as about $3 per share for stock that had sold for as much as $12 a year or so before. Whereas once 52 percent of the stock was controlled by directors and employees, now only 17 percent was owned inside. Only three people owned more than 5 percent; no one owned more than 10 percent except Cogan and Swid. They controlled a whopping 14.2 percent of the place.

That Cogan and Swid were suddenly Sotheby's biggest
investors was not what bothered Brunton. Silent investors are
always welcome in any company; they indicate that people believe they can make money on the place. But these two Americans actually thought they could help out with the operation,
at least according to the statement of identity and purpose they
were required to file by law after their share passed 5 percent,
which they had done on December 14. The two Americans felt
they could help with the finances and with the North American
markets, according to the statement prepared by their banker,
Morgan Grenfell, Inc.

Cogan and Swid of course realized that Brunton would be
upset by their actions. Which was why they had pressed for this
meeting with the board. In America, as shareholders of this
magnitude, they might even win a seat on the board. Obviously
they meant to do more than invest in Sotheby's. "We wanted
to present ourselves as friends of the company who would offer
suggestions. We did not want to take over Sotheby's," Cogan
later said of the meeting. "If only they had listened to us instead of shooting from the hip. We are not bad people, but that's
how Brunton treated us from the beginning."

They had discussed various strategies for weeks before the
fateful meeting. No strangers to the world of take-overs, hostile
or friendly, but practically aliens to the more courtly and complex British system, they sought advice. They found it at one of
London's leading merchant banks, Morgan Grenfell. Founded
in 1828 by George Peabody, an expatriate American who made
his fortune in London, the cornerstone of the Morgan Grenfell
reputation was based on transatlantic deal-making—and still is.
There, inside the handsome Regency marble building in the City
of London, as the financial district is called, Cogan and Swid
met with Roger Seelig, one of the firm's partners.

Seelig warned the two Americans about the possibility of
an anti-Semitic reaction to their bid. The reference was made
fairly obliquely, for he did not want to alienate a potential client.
Sotheby's was still in a lot of trouble, according to the concen-
sus in the City, and the directors were a very touchy group of

people. Brunton had staked his reputation on Sotheby's. Having bungled one important deal at Thomson and, in the opinion of more than a few, having sacrificed the venerable *Times* to the Australian publisher Rupert Murdoch, he needed a big coup under his belt. This is why he was willing to forgo a salary or financial stake in Sotheby's. The problem was that it looked as if he had blown it with Sotheby's as well.

Seelig gave his clients what he thought was sound advice: Buy enough shares in Sotheby's to give yourself a wedge, but do not attempt to force your way in. The two Americans could have launched what's known as a midnight raid of stock in Sotheby's and forced a proxy battle for the remaining shares, whereby shareholders would have to pick sides between GFI/Knoll and Sotheby's. Such a move is called a hostile take-over, for obvious reasons. While in America hostile take-overs had become increasingly common by the early eighties, this was not the case in the U.K., particularly when august firms with close ties to the crown, like Sotheby's, were the prey. A hostile bid may have been out of the question, but a bid by subterfuge was not.

At the December 22 meeting, after Brunton had launched his opening broadside, Cogan and Swid began their presentations. They could see immediately that this was not what you would call a captive audience. Some of the directors seemed to be miles away, their attention having drifted to what they were going to eat for lunch. Neither Cogan nor Swid speaks well in public, but as the better of the two, Swid did most of the talking.

By turns blunt and candid, in his pronounced Bronx accent Swid outlined the achievements of the team in the New York fine-arts world. He told the directors about their various committee memberships. Cogan, he told them, belonged to the prestigious Architecture and Design Committee at the Museum of Modern Art. The word *modern* had a negative impact on the directors, none of them, with the exception of Wolff, having an interest in modern art. (Llewellyn later disdainfully referred to it as "*moduhn* art . . . not a big part of our business.") This was not going well. Swid could see by the looks he was getting that he was being patronized in the worst sort of way. "It was sort of like, go on, finish up, man, let us be through with this."

He then talked about Knoll, the world-ranking manufacturer of modern funriture founded in 1938 to design, produce, and distribute twentieth-century classics. There are probably more pieces by Knoll in the collections of the Museum of Modern Art in New York and the Victoria and Albert in London than by any other twentieth-century manufacturer. The classic cantilevered chrome chair by Marcel Breuer, with cane seat and back—Knoll still produces it. Mies Van Der Rohe—the architect whose Seagram's Building in New York is a monument to the International Style—he had his designs produced by Knoll. Ask any architect or designer about the firm, and they will tell you that it is top drawer.

Unfortunately for Cogan and Swid, the Knoll International label was banned in the U.K., following a lawsuit filed by Parker Knoll, another manufacturer. Again, the directors' eyes began to glaze over. Llewellyn would also later say, "And they *manufacture* steel furniture, for offices, I believe."

As bored as the directors appeared to be by the two Americans' background and current activities, when the time came for Cogan and Swid's recommendations, the board appeared to jump out of their seats with collective rage.

For Cogan and Swid launched a frontal attack on the Brunton regime. Their 14.2 percent interest in Sotheby's, they began firmly, was acquired at prices that "could not be justified by Sotheby's current financial performance." While Brunton began to acquire the appearance of a hungry bulldog, they went on to outline their objective, which was: "that Sotheby's has the necessary financial security to allow its experts to develop the business in the way that they see as the most appropriate and to ensure that this professional staff has the motivation and security of employment fundamental to the establishment of a sound business."

Brunton scoffed at the notion that Cogan and Swid, or GFI/Knoll, could help Sotheby's financial standing, which he insisted was sound in spite of record losses. In meetings with

the press afterward, he would drag out a confusing array of figures on the GFI/Knoll financial standing. "They are a carpet
manufacturer," he said, "with a subsidiary. Eighty million dollars' debt. Twenty-seven million dollars' net worth. Six million
dollars' profit." These figures could never be confirmed,
GFI/Knoll being a privately held company that does not have
to disclose its figures. Moreover, in the months to follow, Cogan
and Swid would effortlessly raise more than $100 million to foot
their bid for Sotheby's.

Cogan and Swid were clearly at odds with Brunton and
everything he was doing to "get this bloody business back on
the track." For their next point was directed at his decision to
cut back building space and lay off employees. "This," they said
bluntly, "appeared to have been motivated by short-term con-
siderations, and little of a constructive nature has been announced to enhance overall growth and development." Brunton
was livid. On occasion, the stock market is a magnificently
democratic place. Imagine being able to throw a few million
dollars into one of Britain's oldest companies and then walk into
the boardroom and tell the future Sir Gordon Brunton that he
has screwed up.

Brunton could not simply ignore these two Americans and
their odius recommendations. As Sotheby's largest shareholders, they had to be reckoned with. So he agreed to approach
the senior experts, and ask them to meet with Cogan and Swid,
who claimed they had new ideas about "creating a more material level of employee participation"—which of course meant
profit-sharing, among other perks.

But Brunton would do so only if Cogan and Swid met his
conditions. He asked them once again to stop buying into Sotheby's, to stop issuing press releases—in brief, to give in to "a
standstill agreement."

Before leaving for New York on the 6:00 P.M. Concorde,
Cogan and Swid told the press what had been discussed in the
meeting. They held back nothing—even their attacks on the
firm's performance were enumerated the next day in the London and New York papers. Brunton of course was livid again.

Cogan and Swid, he later said, had underestimated their adversary. "They said they have great respect for the name Sotheby's, great respect for the working experts, but no respect for the decisions of the management. I am the management. What do you expect me to do?"

SEVEN

THE annual board meeting of Sotheby Parke Bernet, p.l.c., was intimate and cheerful. Even the weather cooperated; it was only February 14, 1983, but already crocuses were peeping out of the ground in Hyde Park. The sun was shining brightly through the windows on the gathering of the entire board of the international outfit, including directors from Europe and America. The walls of the second-floor New Bond Street board-room gave off a deep-green and reassuring glow, the green of pool-table baize, meant to soothe weary souls.

Gordon Brunton led the proceedings with the usual open-ing words about restoring profitability and resurgence of mar-ket interest in works of fine art. There was no mention of Cogan and Swid, but then again no one had heard a peep out of the two Americans since the December 22 meeting and the unfor-tunate subsequent press reports the following day. Instead, Brunton talked about plans to sell the Los Angeles salesroom for $12 million. No one bothered—or dared—to mention that the Los Angeles salesroom had been one of the things Cogan and Swid felt should not be disposed of, primarily because South-ern California was one of the main growth areas of new wealth in the world. Brunton went on to say that in spite of record losses posted for the previous fall and in spite of the market share going to Christie's for the first time in twenty-five years, the future of the firm looked rosy.

Then he showed them why. Around the Chippendale oval table he passed bright color transparencies of star artworks scheduled for sale that spring. There were stunning Degas pastels from the collection of Doris Dick Havemeyer, each worth "in *excess* of a million dollars," he said proudly. From the collection of Sadruddin Aga Khan there were wild African statues and carvings for a special sale in London in the spring. Sadruddin Aga Khan is the half-brother of the late Prince Aly Khan and uncle of the present leader of the Ismaili sect of Islam, the Aga Khan IV. Having grown sentimental in his middle age, Sadruddin was selling his explicit African artworks to free him to pursue only purer Islamic works of art. None of the directors knew very much about African art—a specialist's field with many forgeries and problems—but they all knew the name Khan and agreed that the sale would go well because of the name.

Then there was another name, a name that caused everyone to beam and agree that this one was worth even more money than the other two combined, though no one would have been so vulgar as to say such a thing out loud. The name was Astor, one of the very few words that signifies wealth and breeding both in London and New York circles. There was more to crow about than the name alone. Gavin, second baron Astor of Hever, like the other English titled Astors before him, and like much of titled England according to the old saw, had always sold exclusively through Christie's. For reasons that would unfold over the next few minutes, Astor had decided to sell both Hever Castle and its contents through Sotheby's.

As to why Lord Astor had decided to switch ponies at this of all times—when Sotheby's was down and Christie's was up—Brunton would only intimate as the directors looked at pictures of the suits of armor from Hever Castle. It was no secret that Sotheby's real estate division, founded by Wilson and Cave in New York a few years back, had snared the castle as one of its main listings of the year. Christie's did not sell real estate. This was the main reason Astor had moved over to Sotheby's. Hever Castle, as nearly every student knows, is one of the most important Tudor buildings, not so much for its design—although the castle comes complete with moat and crenelated ramparts, storybook style—but rather for its link to a tragic and romantic epoch in English history. For Hever was the ancestral home of Anne Boleyn—second wife of Henry VIII and mother of the future Queen Elizabeth I—who was beheaded on perhaps trumped-up charges of adultery.

Since 1903 the castle had been the seat of the English branch of the Astor family and cornerstone of its curious place in English aristocracy. For the Astors are not English or even British. John Jacob Astor, the founder of the vast fortune that made his name synonymous with wealth, was a German who emigrated from Frankfurt to America in 1783. On his death in 1848, having turned a business in fur pelts into one of the largest and most diverse fortunes in America, he was considered the richest of the rich. In 1890 his great-grandson William Waldorf Astor moved a sizable portion of the fortune to England, where he bought his way into the aristocracy. He did so by investing in huge tracts of land and by renovating Hever Castle, which had fallen into serious disrepair, to the tune of 13 million in 1903 dollars.

Soon thereafter he was given the title Viscount Astor, the feather in the cap he had sought when he embarked on his lavish spending spree, "impelled," according to one account, "by history." To the 3,000-acre estate, Astor added a mock Tudor village of 114 houses, cottages, and flats. Family and friends occupied the main castle, where the rooms were renamed in keeping with the tragic past: the King Henry VIII office and bedroom, the Anne of Cleves (she lived there too) sitting room, the Anne Boleyn bedroom with "adjacent bath and WC with gold-plated fittings," and Lady Astor's bedroom "with direct access to the tower." Guests and staff stayed across the moat in the Tudor village. It was a veritable Arthurian theme park before the notion of theme parks existed, one of the first erected by history-hungry Americans, although Lord Astor was by then more English than the English.

Gavin Astor, who inherited the fortune and title Baron Astor of Hever in 1971, was forced to begin selling off major pieces of the family's holdings by 1976. That was the year that he sold *The Times* of London to The Thomson Organisation, and met Gordon Brunton, the president of the Canadian-based conglomerate. By 1982, Gavin, having soberly faced the financial prospect of continuing the medieval charade at Hever, decided to unload the whole show: the valuable suits of armor, the lances and crossbows, the portraits of Tudor personages, the castle, mock Tudor village, and 3,000-acre estate within an hour's drive of London. Edward Cave, the head of the real estate division of Sotheby's who had married into the Astor family, contacted Lord Astor as soon as he heard of his decision. Once again Sotheby's connections in the upper classes had paid off; moreover, Gavin, having worked with Brunton on the sale of *The Times*, felt he had another valuable contact at Sotheby's.

The directors were thrilled by the prospect of an Astor sale in their dealing rooms. The name alone would surely bring out the valuable status seekers Sotheby's so avidly courts, and the sale of the castle would also begin a new chapter in Sotheby's International Realty Corporation, one of the few profitable divisions of the firm that year. The meeting concluded with strong India tea and heart-shaped cookies, it being Valentine's Day. Brunton was pleased to see that Sotheby's was shaping up under his guidance, or so he thought. Death may not have been good to Sotheby's, but the firm had found a friend in inflation and downward mobility. Poor Lord Astor might be losing his fortune, but with Sotheby's in charge of the dispersal, at least he would get maximum press coverage of the sad day. When asked what his favorite was among the many treasures in the castle, Astor would lift off his half-glasses and say, unctuously, "I loved the little casket" (a small fourteenth-century carved ivory box).

Sotheby's largest single shareholder was not present at the Valentine's Day meeting. GFI was not even told of the meeting. Nor did Brunton mention the "felt fellows from New Jersey," as he had started calling Cogan and Swid. Brunton's and Sotheby's banker, Hugh Stevenson of Warburg's, believed that the

firm could weather this take-over threat. This was one reason
for the show of colored pictures in the Valentine's Day meeting.
The message was: business as usual in spite of all that was
going on.

Brunton "did most of the talking in the meeting," Marion
recalls. "I don't believe we were even asked questions. It was,
here is what's for sale, and here are the figures, and here is
how my scheme is falling into place." Brunton wanted to believe he had averted a Cogan and Swid take-over, or any other
unwanted take-over. Little did he realize that his directors had
plans of their own for the future of the firm. While they sat
munching their cookies and sipping their tea, some were plan-
ning their own coups d'état against this Caesar in their midst.

Brunton prided himself on his good word, and since Cogan
and Swid had asked him to arrange meetings for them with the
senior experts, he would follow through on his promise. Soon
after the first of the year he began to ask senior experts whether
they would like to meet with Cogan and Swid. He gleefully reported back that no one had agreed to meet with them, that
they had concurred with his assessment of the "felt fellows."
There was, he insisted, no "synergy" between GFI/Knoll and
Sotheby's, no reason for further talks. Although some of the
directors later complained that they had been bullied into saying no to a meeting, Brunton insisted such talk was "nonsense.
I asked them, and they said no."

From their penthouse offices above Manhattan, Cogan and
Swid were not deterred in the least by Brunton's obstinance. In
fact, as Swid later recalled, "We felt motivated by his challenge. If he wouldn't work with us, we thought, we would work
without him." The problem was a matter of timing more than
anything else. They had not yet announced that they intended
to launch a proxy battle to win controlling interest in Sotheby's, but were quietly preparing for the day they would join
battle.

First they set up a war chest to finance their bid. This being
the beginning of the great age of leveraged buy-outs in America, borrowing the money was no great feat. Leveraged buy-outs,
a controversial lending scheme used primarily for American deals

and thus fairly alien to the likes of Brunton or Warburg's, are quite simple in theory. On the assumption that the lender will succeed in buying out the shareholders, the banks will lend nearly all the money needed for the take-over and will base their calculations not on the assets of the lender but rather on the assets, or future worth, of the prey. Brunton would of course later claim that Cogan and Swid were borrowing heavily against the uncertain future of Sotheby's, and that if they failed, Sotheby's would end up in the hands of the banks.

All of which was true, as far as it went.

It was not difficult, for starters, to convince Citibank of the attractiveness of an involvement in a Sotheby's take-over. Within weeks Citibank had loaned GFI/Knoll most of the $100 million needed to launch their bid. For Citibank, this was more than another loan. For several years, America's second-largest bank had eyed investments in works of art as an attractive alternative to conventional stocks and bonds. In fact, the bank had once entered into an advisory agreement with Sotheby's in the late seventies. Although the Citibank/Sotheby's art-investment scheme did not work out, there was no reason why some other scheme could not work out in the future, especially with Citibank holding the purse strings in the new Sotheby's.

On the weight of the Citibank commitment, Cogan and Swid were able to persuade two other banks to put up smaller loans. These were Crocker Bank in San Francisco and Manufacturers Hanover Trust in New York. To these banks, whose rationale for a Sotheby's loan was a more conventional matter without any special interest, Cogan and Swid made a compelling presentation. They pointed to Sotheby's figures over the past few years, and told the bankers how they could be improved. There was no reason, the two Americans argued, why the firm should not post earnings of up to $20 million a year in good years. In fact, even in the best years Sotheby's profits had slumped downward while volume climbed upward, never exceeding $7 million.

There was absolutely nothing new about Sotheby's carrying a huge debt burden. Even the acquisition of Parke-Bernet, as Wilson and Pollen could well remember, was financed by the friendly Morgan Guaranty Trust loan officer; and most of the subsequent expansion programs had been financed outside the firm on rather flimsy collateral. "The price of art will only go up," Wilson had repeated over and over, like a priest attempting to convert the wayward. He buttressed his argument with reams of statistics, published in conjunction with standard-bearers like *The Times* of London, charting the progress of such investibles as netsukes and Dürer prints. Even paperweights were bought and sold as though they were pork bellies.

The *problem* with a service industry like Sotheby's is that the assets go down in the elevator each night—the assets being the experts who sniff out and appraise works of art. So even the most modest loan becomes a big burden on the balance sheet, showing up, as it does, as a debit with nothing to protect the creditor against sudden default. Say you lend Sotheby's $10 million, hypothetically speaking. Even though Sotheby's stock is valued at $100 million, the real value of the firm— that is, of its holdings in quickly convertible property—is only $20 million, the worth of Sotheby's meager holdings in real estate, most of its property being leased. If suddenly the price of art does not go up, you may be stuck with a loan that is very difficult to collect.

EIGHT

"Did you hear the news?"
"What?"
"Florence died last night."
  Pause
"What's in the will?"

Alight frost covered the grounds at Château de Clavary the morning after Florence La Caze Gould died. Peter Wilson, Gould's main adviser in her lavish spending sprees for more than thirty years, glanced across the Picasso mosaic mural lining the hallway to the frozen garden outside, and placed another phone call.

As if he were preparing to move the oversized chess-piece sculptures arranged in military formation on the lawn of the hillside compound, Wilson's mind worked in terms of major strategy. There was nothing small about this morning's prey. A member of the enormously rich American Gould family, whose excesses are said to have sparked the term *robber baron*, Florence must have invested her entire fortune in art, antiques, jewelry, and no telling what else.

The Gould estate would breathe new life into the firm. Some said she had $200 million, maybe more, invested in her possessions, nearly half the total revenue of Sotheby's the year before. And nearly everyone knew that "Florence was a Sotheby's kind of person," and that Wilson had been her main link to the oldest auction house in the English-speaking world.

He consulted his gold Patek Philippe wristwatch: 7:30 A.M., March 1, 1983. The art market, so small yet so international, made communications a constant battle against time zones. Too early to call New York, Wilson thought, where it was only 1:30 A.M. He had already called everyone in London worth talking with about the matter. He had already phoned his Associated Press contact about the obituary, feeding all the right information, at least for his purposes. No doubt everyone would read about her death and life in the afternoon papers, her secrets going to the grave with her.

What to do?

He studied his reflection in a mirror as he phoned to his driver. His own reflection had been a great source of comfort over the years, and today was no exception. Unmistakably English and aristocratic, just dissipated enough for no one to mistake him for a Hun, he was the ideal person, he had always thought, for the head of Sotheby's. Those two Americans, however, looked nothing like what a Sotheby's auctioneer should. He had already used this to his advantage when he spoke with that nice Stephen Swid over the phone. He had made it clear that he would work with them if they succeeded, but that they were not the type to head Sotheby's. "Yes, fine, come for the weekend," he had said, "but don't let's go to bed together."

Speeding down the hill from the château in the back of the Rolls-Royce Silver Cloud he had brought with him when he retired two years before, Wilson cursed the cold this morning. Having looked forward most of his life to the warmth of his beloved Côte d'Azur hideaway at Auribeau-sur-Siagne, he grumbled whenever the thermometer dropped below sixty degrees Fahrenheit. As the car glided effortlessly down N-85 from Grasse into Cannes, past the tatty high-rise hotels and holiday camps that had spoiled much of the region, Florida- and California-style, he wondered whether the low cloud cover would burn away by midday. Florence, he thought, would have been pleased by the solemnity of her death day.

There was no need to give the driver directions; he knew the way by heart. Each week for the past three years, and as frequently as possible for years before, Wilson or someone from his household had made the thirty-minute trip from Château de Clavary to El Patio, the first house on the beach at Cannes. There was little to talk about as the years rolled on, and he had come to hate his visits with her. Many of their mutual friends, like Somerset Maugham and Douglas Cooper, had died already. So there was little to gossip about except the ailments of the infirm and aged. They could always talk about things, both being obsessed by rare and beautiful objects, although their tastes were markedly different. In sharp contrast to the refined elegance of the neoclassical Château de Clavary, El Patio, behind its wrought-iron grillwork, brimmed with an overflow of exotica gathered from all over the world to please no one but Florence.

Some would call her a collector. To the French government, the long-standing American expatriate was a patron of the arts, having presented $2,000 a year to writers through the Prix Florence Gould. She belonged to the Académie des Beaux Arts, and even paid her income taxes from time to time with the gift of a painting, as only France would allow, in lieu of cash. Her close friends, a gay assortment, mostly of men her age who shared her taste for gilt and blue rinse or henna, knew she was neither. She was, in the words of the Dowager Marchioness of Dufferin and Ava, "just another rich American who fancied gaudy jewels."

Even in her eighty-seventh and final year of lusty abandon, Gould could not satisfy her urge for more. Hiding behind thick drapery that shut out most of the Mediterranean sun, her trademark dark-blue sunglasses taking care of the rest, Gould had summoned new treasures into her inner sanctum. She lived like an opium smoker, and in fact, many of her decadent aristocratic friends were opium smokers.

Wilson had recently arranged the sale of some of Florence's jewelry through Sotheby's in Zurich, but he was not sure what she had picked up with the proceeds of the sale.

Perhaps it was a rhinoceros.

No doubt it was fashioned from porcelain, elaborated with a gilt gold mount or handles or both, probably from the eighteenth century, though more than a few less-desirable nineteenth-century bibelots had crept into her mad assembly. Unless it was an ashtray or cigarette lighter, it was probably useless. Even the rococo clocks she had bought failed to keep proper time. There was a time when Wilson would have had a mental inventory of her vast array of possessions, but that time had long since slipped away.

Florence Gould was famous for her jewelry. The late Shah of Iran called the Gould jewels the only rival to the Persian collection. Nearly everyone left El Patio with a jewelry story. Covered literally head to toe in diamonds, rubies, emeralds, sapphires, pearls—clips in her hair and on her shoes—she would perambulate into breakfast smiling regally, even after nights of epic debaucheries. Then there was the time she rode into the Cambodian jungle during the height of the Khmer Rouge reign of terror that ended in one of the worst holocausts in modern times. Perched atop an elephant, with jewels dripping off the side of the howdah, she smiled and waved to the natives, as they appeared spellbound by the spectacle of this bejeweled madwoman.

Then there were the Gould paintings. Paintings being the most difficult, not to mention costly, art objects to collect, Gould had a tougher time making the big splash she wanted in this field. John Richardson, the English art critic who now lives in New York, remembers meeting Gould in the late fifties when she had begun her famous foray into the world of art. "She could not say no. She would buy anything that caught her fancy, beginning with a whole room of junk by the late Bernard Buffet, who was then very fashionable in certain circles but later fell rapidly from favor in all circles." Even her dealer and longtime friend, Daniel Wildenstein, admits he had to guide her buying to avoid lapses in taste: "She would buy," he said, "anything I told her to."

But with all the Gould money injected into the art market, she was bound to walk away with some premier examples, in spite of her indiscriminate taste. There was the large collection of post-Impressionist paintings by Pierre Bonnard. Purchased presumably because Wildenstein told her to, the Bonnards eventually climbed in value and in generally accepted historical opinion—even though when she bought them, Bonnard was considered second tier to his better-known contemporaries, like Henri Matisse and Claude Monet, and almost no one had considered collecting his works. There was also a masterwork by Vincent van Gogh that almost redeemed her eye in the opinion of some critics. Titled *"Paysage au Soleil Levant,"* the large oil on canvas of a rising sun over a field of wheat in the Provence region of France was purchased in the early 1960s for more than a million dollars—an enormous sum then for an artwork—from J. Robert Oppenheimer, one of the men credited with the invention of the atom bomb. She hung the picture by her breakfast table; and she called it variously "my friend" or "one of my best friends."

Life did not begin this way for Florence La Caze Gould; and Wilson, like any good dealer/consort, was willing to go along with her grandiloquent charade as though she were to the manor born. There were no diamonds outlining her bassinette when she was born in 1895. Her father was a publisher who sent his wife and only child ahead of him to resettle in Paris in 1906.

Some say Florence was an actress. Others insist she was an opera singer, as she, too, liked to claim when asked about her past. By the time she became the third Mrs. Frank Jay Gould in 1923, there was little wonder why the cruel would say in a whisper that she had been a café concert chanteuse. Florence was not the first show girl the terribly spoiled youngest son of Jay Gould had lavished jewels upon. Nor was she the first short buxom blonde to capture his attention. Unlike the others, however, she was by his side from the time he turned forty-five to his death at seventy-eight years old.

France was full of expatriate Americans during the twenties, but the Frank Jay Goulds did not mingle with Sara and Gerald Murphy or the F. Scott Fitzgeralds, even though Florence would later claim to have led a literary circle from the time of her marriage to Gould. Their literary contribution, rather, would be their life, as loosely novelized later on by the French novelist André Gide in *The Immoralist,* a shocking account of the decadent bourgeoisie. He raced horses. She wore jewels. He built casinos. She was the first woman to wear pajama-suits in public, exclusively designed, so the story goes, for Florence. She wanted to carry her blackjack chips in pants pockets.

By 1932 the Frank Goulds owned more gambling casinos than anyone in the world and continued to build the Gould fortune, despite the worldwide Depression, through their casino and real estate investments. Their great achievement, the Palais Méditerrané, covered two acres of marble, bronze, crystal, and velour at Nice, and turned the Côte d'Azur into a fashionable summer resort. Home base for the merry gambling Goulds was the sleepy fishing village of Juan-les-Pins, where Frank developed another more exclusive and luxurious resort. There, midway between Cannes and Monte Carlo, guests gambled all night and water-skied all day, sleeping god-only-knows-when, confident in the knowledge that they were in the fast lane. The Goulds maintained matching speedboats, each named for their respective nicknames for the other: *Gay Boy*, for the devil-may-care Frank; *Putti*, for the voluptuous Florence. The childless couple also kept his and hers Pekingese dogs, similarly named.

Florence raced her Hispano-Suiza up and down the Mediterranean coastline nearly every day, often rigged out in so much jewelry that she "positively glistened," according to one admirer. Long after Frank, who was nearly twenty years older than she, had gone to bed, Florence would wander the casino like a silk-pajamaed Jezebel, her pockets filled with gambling chips, her ruby-red lips forced into a moue, the trademark dark-blue sunglasses hiding what was going on in her eyes. When the war drove most sensible people out of the Riviera—including Frank Gould, who sailed home to his family's estate near Ardsley, New York—Florence remained behind in Juan-les-Pins and, as she

later put it, "made do." Even though the fast lane she so loved
had changed course by then, Florence continued her wander-
ings of the casino. Only now she was accompanied by handsome
blond SS officers who were rigged out in black uniforms, red
swastikas on their upper arms, and shiny knee-high boots.

Making do meant more to Florence than merely surviving.
With at least one of the officers, whom we will call Jerlof von
Click to protect the identity of his son, Florence had a pro-
tracted love affair that lasted most of the war. After his return
to Germany, Von Click had a son in 1952 and named Florence
his godmother. Years later, when the godson met his godmother
for the first time in Cannes, she greeted him warmly and immediately told him what had taken place between his father and
herself during the war. The godson found the confession in-
credible, not so much because he believed his father incapable
of having an affair but because Florence had told him about it
so hastily and indiscreetly. Sometime later he stumbled across
pictures of his father in uniform in the arms of the buxom millionairess, and then he knew it had been true.

After the war the Gould name came up in connection with
Nazi sympathizers in an exposé in *The Washington Post*. It was
discovered that funds from a Gould bank account had been
funneled into an SS account in Monte Carlo in 1942, 1943, and
1945. The addled Florence claimed she had done so only to
protect her husband's investments in the South of France and
had no contact with the SS during the war. The Nazis, she insisted, had told her they would seize all Gould property if she
did not make contributions. The case was dropped within a year,
and as far as can be told, never reopened.

Florence was just the type of client Wilson wanted to develop as a "Sotheby's kind of person," and he brought her into
the fold with an invitation to the first evening auction since the
eighteenth century, the October 1958 sale of the collection of
the late Jakob Goldschmidt. Florence loved the excitement of
the salesroom nearly as much as she had loved the excitement
of the gambling rooms at Juan-les-Pins, although at first she
merely sat back and watched without bidding on anything
important. The auction rooms added a thrill to an other-

wise scholarly cerebral world, and Florence was still seeking the final *frisson* even as she became known as a patron of the arts.

Wilson was not alone in his pursuit of the Gould legacy. Every gigolo, con man, pretender, art dealer, and hustler in the South of France, probably even stretching across the Mediterranean to North Africa, wanted in on the Gould franchise. Fortunately for the man from Sotheby's, there was only one other serious contender. He was Daniel Wildenstein, the leading art dealer in Paris, and a long-standing friend of the Goulds' through horse-racing circles in Deauville. Wildenstein became her trustee, her art adviser, and head of the foundation he had her set up as the main beneficiary of her estate: the Florence J. Gould Foundation. "Daniel," she would tell friends, "is like a son to me." Wildenstein would say after her death that Florence had been "like a surrogate mother to me."

As the trustee and director of the Florence J. Gould Foundation, which was set up in the sixties, Wildenstein would not be able to fulfill his duties to the estate and at the same time dispose of the Gould treasury of art objects and jewelry. Although few people knew this, Wilson did. So he continued hotly to pursue the Gould legacy even after it became clear that Wildenstein would be her main supplier.

Wilson had to endure dinners, course after course, served by a staff of ten, throughout which Florence would drink Cognac and chain-smoke Lucky Strike cigarettes. One frequent guest in the sixties recalls that she made no effort to mix sexes, most of her parties consisting of men her age who had never married. After dinner, the guest recalls, Florence would sometimes play what the others began to call "a game of show-and-tell." Having ingested enough Cognac to fortify a men's club, she would turn to whoever was on her right and say stentoriously, "You wanna see some pearls?" The guest would say yes, even if he had been put through the ritual before, and with a flourish she would clap her hands together, as though she were summoning Nubian slaves.

Three or four male servants would then appear, holding stacks of English Dundee cake tins in outstretched arms. Slowly and with great display she would reach for the first tin, open the lid carefully, and move her pudgy fingers inside. The candlelight made it difficult for some to see what happened next, but before long everyone could hear the sound of birdseed running through her fingers and spilling off the table, like grain through a sieve. A pearl necklace would surface and Florence would wave it around once or twice, spinning the strand around her middle finger, before handing it to the guest on her right to pass counterclockwise to the others around the Louis XV dinner table.

Florence believed that birdseed would preserve the luster of pearls, long after most sensible people had discovered pearl-keepers, the humidorlike boxes recommended by jewelers. A harmless eccentricity, this. Keeping strands of pearls white by storing them in birdseed in old, used cake tins was just the sort of thing one would expect from this aging American who had lost track of time in the sunny South of France, long after her Cheri and last of her Cheris had gone for good. It was her link with the glorious past, and no one would deny her that.

"Florence's pearls," a guest once exclaimed after a game of show-and-tell, "could form a cable from Le Havre to New York!" And everyone laughed and laughed and laughed and laughed.

Everything Florence owned had meant something to her. Wilson's mind raced as he thought about a mind that could keep all this in place. Standing outside the wrought-iron grillwork that had inspired someone to call the place El Patio, he remembered what had gone on inside over the years. He remembered how Florence had looked the first time he met her: short, buxom, radiant jet-black hair coiffed perfectly in place, like a black helmet, her dark glasses seeming somehow fitting on her even in the middle of the London winter in 1955, or was it 1956? He thought about where Sotheby's had been and where it was going. He thought about where he had been and where he was going. For a man accustomed to death in the morning, Florence's had touched him like an electric jolt.

A smell of sulfur rose from the Mediterranean; the sea of the ancients that was now too polluted to swim in, at least on this fashionable part of the coastline. A train passed right by the house, feet away from where he was standing. His brow wrinkled as his head stooped more than usual. Perhaps it was time to turn Sotheby's over to someone new. Florence had come to him at the beginning of it all. She had bought and bought and bought. And now that she was gone, there would be the sale of the century. There was a certain symmetry in this, and he was not the only one to identify it as such. But first there was the sale to think about. This was his account, and he would be certain to take something off the top for bringing it into the house.

As the car rose gently back up the hill to Château de Clavary, where peace and order would be restored, Wilson recalled what he knew about the Gould estate. Florence had always told him, admittedly after some prompting on his part, that she wanted to make a "big splash" with the sale of her possessions. "The only regret I have," she had once told him after a talk about the sale, "is that I will not be around to see the looks on everyone's faces." This was a comforting thought, and he did not allow himself to think of the possibility that she had said it as a come-on to make sure he returned to visit her.

There were no heirs. The French government would probably cream the top of the art collection for death duties, and the American government would want its share too, only in cash. Though the Goulds lived in France for most of the century, they kept their money safely in the United States in an old-line bank known as U.S. Trust Company, the bank the court had appointed as trustee after Frank successfully sued his family trust in the twenties.

After death duties had been paid, there was no telling how much of the estate would be left for Sotheby's. But Wilson had some idea of the amount. Having handled the sale over the past few years of some of her lesser pieces of jewelry, he knew that the estate was cash-poor. Though it might be rich in assets, there was very little left in the way of stocks or bonds. Florence would not have sold a thing if she had not needed the money. There was at least $200 million, he thought confidently to himself, tied up in artworks, furnishings, and jewelry, the largest single estate he had ever come across. Surely, he figured, she would have stipulated in her will that Sotheby's hold the sale. Surely she would not have forgotten her old friend Peter Wilson, *cher Pierre*, and all the times he had dined at El Patio and held her hand when she was beside herself.

The prospect of a big Gould blockbuster sale, as Sotheby's called the biggest of the big, charged him with new purpose, and he noticed, as the car swung into the drive under an alley of plane trees, that the sun had finally come out. There might even be a sunset warming the green hills of the Côte d'Azur. It was finally time to call New York: He placed the overseas call himself, waiting patiently the two or three minutes it took for the fuzzy connection to be completed. He was calling John Young, the co-executor, along with Wildenstein, of Gould's estate, in his New York office, the Wall Street offices of Cahill, Gordon & Reindel. *An odd choice, Cahill, Gordon*, Wilson thought to himself. He had never heard of anyone rich having their legal work done there. Most rich Americans, at least in his experience, preferred old-line WASP firms like Millbank, Tweed, Hadley & McCloy; Shearman & Sterling; or Cravath, Swaine & Moore. Had he looked in the *American Lawyer Guidebook*, which he probably did not, he would have found Cahill, Gordon described as "a bunch of tough Irish litigators." The choice would not have seemed so odd. For Jay Gould was nothing if not a tough litigator himself.

"Hello, Mr. Young, this is Peter Wilson from Sotheby's." He spoke firmly into the receiver to compensate for the static sound common in overseas calls. "I was so sorry to learn about Florence's death this morning. She was a very, very dear friend of mine, and of Sotheby's. I will miss her and I want you to know that I am here if there is anything I can do to help you."

Unfortunately, Wilson had not met Young, or at least he did not remember having done so. Young was the latest executor in a long line of Cahill, Gordon partners appointed by the firm to handle Gould's affairs. Wilson had met many of them over the years, but Florence had outlived all but Young.

"Yes, well, um, thank you for calling." Young spoke wistfully in a barely audible tone. "It is a very depressing day, very depressing. We are going to miss Florence very much. You know, I was just with her recently, and she seemed fine. The whole thing is very disturbing. We will call you when we need you. Good-bye."

Wilson did not ask whether Sotheby's had been named in the will. He knew from past experience that it was too early to ask such a direct question. Young did not offer any leading information either. This was the first time he had dealt with the auction houses on a sale of this type, and he was not yet sure what to say. Wilson was right about at least one thing: Cahill, Gordon was an odd choice for a person like Florence—not, as it turned out, that it would be a bad choice.

Moments after Wilson called, Stephen Lash, the executive vice-president at Christie's on Park Avenue, phoned to offer his condolences. Lash could hardly claim to have been a close friend of Gould's, but that did not seem to matter. Young handled this call with the same response. He placed the phone back on the receiver and looked through the plate-glass wall of his skyscraper office to the East River opposite Wall Street. *Sotheby's and Christie's,* he thought. But wasn't Sotheby's in big trouble these days? Hadn't he read something?

Peter Cecil Wilson, Commander of the British Empire,
architect of the modern auction spectacle—and of
the theory "The price of art will only go up"
—behind the podium at Sotheby's in London

Typical Sotheby's clientele

(left) Paloma Picasso and Gregory Peck   *(above)* Ann
Getty, unidentified woman, decorator Mario Buatta,
and Oscar de la Renta   *(below)* Bob Guccione and friend
Kathy Keaton

More typical Sotheby's clientele

(far left) Baron Hans Thyssen-Bornemisza
(left) Anonymous bidders   *(above)* Bianca Jagger with
friend Thomas Ammann

SOTHEBY PARKE BERNET

Julian Thompson, Sotheby's London president, who told
Cogan and Swid: "You are not our kind of Americans."

James Lally, John Marion, and Michael Ainslie

(above) Sotheby's London office used this photo to promote a sale of contemporary art which included this "piece of Alan Jones sculpture." At right is Lucy Havelock-Allan, the new specialist in the field at the time of the sale. She built up the business in a matter of months.   *(above right)* Hever Castle, including inner and outer moats, Anne Boleyn's garden, and mock Tudor village   *(far right)* Florence La Caze Gould in famous trademark blue sunglasses and pearls

A. Alfred and Judy Taubman enter Sotheby's salesroom for
a gala party shortly after Judy told *Vanity Fair* that Alfred
was "much thinner, thank you."

Henry Ford II hangs on to his good friend A. Alfred
Taubman.

John Marion pulls a bid from the air in the Gould sale of paintings in April 1985. At left is Vincent van Gogh's *Paysage au Soleil Levant*, which Sotheby's claims to have sold for $9.9 million, though no one knows who bought it.

(above) Marshall and Maureen Cogan out for a rare evening
in dinner clothes   (below) Steve and Nan Swid

NINE

BERNARD Combemale threw back the Porthault sheets on his antique French bed. He descended slowly from the bed to the antique Persian rug, feet first over the side rail, sinking toes into the softness of one of the many valuable rugs that cushioned the floors of the Fifth Avenue apartment he had lived in since his marriage. It was only 5:00 A.M. on a cold and blustery February morning in 1983, and no one else was up, not even the staff of eight.

There was no need to tiptoe about. He was not going to awaken anybody. His wife, Pamela, the Woolworth fortune heiress, would probably sleep until noon in her own room under her own set of Porthault linens, down the hall. The children were away at school. In buildings like this one, there was no reason to worry about disturbing the neighbors, even when your neighbors who shared the same elevator bank and layout—the layout the press said was worth $8 million—were Claus and Sunny von Bülow, of New York and Newport. The Von Bülows would not be up anyway. Sunny was in a coma. Claus was in Newport, gathering evidence for his defense, having been accused by his stepchildren of attempting to murder Sunny by

injecting her with insulin. Combemale thought Von Bülow was
guilty, and like most of New York society, he would tell you so
if you asked him, opinions about the Von Bülow case being valued dinner-table baggage.

Combemale was not up at this ungodly hour to discuss Von
Bülow. He was up and seated in his walnut-paneled study, facing dark Central Park, because of the blasted time zones. For
the next few hours he would conduct business in Europe and
Great Britain, it being already midmorning across the Atlantic.
Priority on this morning's agenda was the future of Sotheby's,
as his good friend Peter Wilson had described the deal to him
a few weeks back. For the French-born Combemale was an international banker, independently employed of course, who had
found, as his good friends often teased him, "a million dollar
baby in a five and ten cent store."

Life had been easier when the Combemales resided in
Monaco. Bernard had a good job as director of the Société des
Bains de Mer, the official chamber of commerce in the princi-
pality, where he drummed up business for Monte Carlo. The
Combemales traveled with the royal family. Pamela, who had
as her role model her aunt Barbara Hutton, loved the gambling
and water-skiing fast life she found there. Bernard, who as a
young man had been one of the handsomest playboys in the international set that revolved around tiger-striped booths in El
Morocco in New York and in the casinos in Monte Carlo, enjoyed being back in one of the haunts of his youth, even as his
temples turned gray and his belly soft.

Then a certain breach of protocol occurred. In Monaco,
where the royal family earns part of its yearly income from staged
appearances for the French and international press, appearance is everything. The Combemales, especially Bernard, packed
their Vuitton bags and departed Monaco for the apartment in
New York, where they would begin life all over again.

Back in the land of the second chance, Bernard wasted little time. Fortunately for him, there were good friends willing to
help him out in his new business venture. Not that he needed
to work, but he did not want to end up like Von Bülow, the
husband whose $25,000-a-year income could not even pay his

own way to the tailor. Did he? So Roy Cohn, the divorce lawyer whose notoriety came early when he served as an associate
to Senator Joseph McCarthy during the Commie-bashing fifties,
sent some banking work to Combemale. Recently Combemale
had been dealing in Belgian trucking companies and helping
Frenchmen frightened of François Mitterand's brand of social-
ism find investments in the United States under Ronald Reagan's laissez-faire form of capitalism. Then the call came in from
Wilson, about "zeez Cogans and Swids," as Combemale described the unwanted suitors and largest shareholders of "Sussebee's," in his charmingly French-accented English.

He worked hard on the Sotheby's deal. By turns in rapid,
staccato French and Maurice Chevalier English, speaking over
the telephone, leaning over the table at Le Cirque or Morti-
mer's, buttonholing an important contact behind a potted palm
in the lobby of the Plaza, Bernard Combemale was, as one friend
put it, "one thousand and one places at once." Sotheby's was
his kind of deal: glamorous, exciting, a change of pace from
Belgian trucking companies, a chance to get back into the circle
of the rich and their furniture that had all but shut him out.

Wilson had not asked the board of directors for permis-
sion to contact Combemale. Although Brunton and Hugh Stevenson, the banker from Warburg's, had told the other directors
that they would take care of the problem, by February nearly
everyone knew that they had not. At least Wilson knew. Under
a normal take-over battle plan, Warburg's, as Sotheby's de-
fending banker, would scour the landscape for a new and more
acceptable buyer, a White Knight, in the Arthurian parlance of
the take-over world. There was no harm, Wilson figured, in doing
a little scouring of his own. Wilson was not the only director to
think this way, but his actions produced the most fruitful results.

John Marion was dialing for dollars too. Marion contacted
Henry McNeil, the president of McNeil Laboratories, home of
Tylenol, whose recent sale of the lab to Johnson & Johnson had
flushed the ultraconservative collector of American antiques with
a surplus of cash. McNeil was Marion's type of person: down
to earth, crusty, not given to fancy words or affectations. But

McNeil was not sure he wanted to get involved with a small firm as troublesome as Sotheby's. Marion also found other numbers on his Rolodex. Like William Agee, the whiz kid who had recently averted a take-over while at the helm of Bendix on the part of Martin Marietta. The take-over involved far greater sums of money than the Sotheby's deal, and Agee had become a sort of folk hero, until he met his Goliath too. Jealous associates accused him of promoting Mary Cunningham through the ranks only because the two were having an affair. Cunningham left in a cloud of smoke that interested woman's liberationists. Agee left in 1983. Marion found Agee his type of person, too, but there was little the two men could do together for the future of Sotheby's.

Other names had been publicly circulated as prospective buyers for Sotheby's. David Murdoch, the California financier, art collector, and one of Sotheby's largest shareholders already, was one name that cropped up. Murdoch claims such talk was mere speculation, based on the arithmetic involved in his holdings in Sotheby's stock. Even Bob Guccione was mentioned as a possible suitor. Although the publisher of *Penthouse* magazine owns an impressive collection of old masters and modern art, and amazes traditional auction-goers from time to time with his show of gold chains framed by an open-necked shirt collar, he said he had no interest in acquiring Sotheby's. One of the most frequently cited names was American Express, the credit card company that had branched out in recent years into the world of high finance and luxury goods. Here was a perfect marriage for Sotheby's, a high-finance luxury-goods outfit itself. Before Cogan and Swid arrived on the take-over scene, Sanford Weill, the president of Shearson/American Express, and Cogan's nemesis, had said he had no interest in Sotheby's. "All this upper-class English gentleman stuff," he was quoted as saying. "I just don't get it."

Sotheby's was for sale even before Cogan and Swid had bought into the place, and Combemale knew that this fact was on his side. All he would have to do would be to come up with a willing buyer—almost any buyer, it seemed, would do. He had no specific instructions about religion or class background, but with his pedigree, Wilson could trust him to find a suitable replacement for Cogan and Swid.

Like the good investment banker that he is, Combemale knew how to put the deal into motion. Using the background information he had been supplied by Wilson and Sotheby's annual reports, he prepared a fifteen-page double-spaced typewritten prospectus for sale, bound in a plastic sleeve. The report covered the basic financial, management, and marketing information on Sotheby's as it stood then, with a few pages devoted to the future of the firm, which was covered in the most general terms, since Combemale did not want to be held responsible for unfulfilled prophecies. He was, after all, a banker, not a clairvoyant. The report was then circulated to a select number of prospects with enough money and interest in art collecting to justify buying into Sotheby's.

Combemale left no stone unturned. Even those who had already been mentioned as likely candidates received copies of the report. There was no time to lose, and every reason to snare a White Knight before the next guy did. Once word gets out in the small and tightly knit investment banking world, everyone wants to get in on the deal. Even in the case of Sotheby's, a small firm by international standards, five bankers, including Combemale, would eventually take part of the pie home with them. Should he fail, then he would have wasted his time and effort for nothing, except perhaps the chance of another deal spinning off from this one.

The first call came in to his answering service from Steve Ross, the jazzy chairman of Warner Communications, which (more to the point) owned Atari Video Games. Warner Communications had been cited as a possible buyer of Sotheby's as early as 1979, when the firm was flush with earnings from the boom in video. It would have been a perfect match for Ross, too, an art collector himself who wanted in on the auction-room game. Sotheby's was not then interested in an alliance with Ross; and by the time the frightened auction house was willing to reopen talks, Atari had fallen on hard times and Warner was looking for people to take the video outfit off its hands. That was what Ross called to tell Combemale, opening the possibility of another sale for the entrepreneur but not the possibility he was after at the moment.

The second call came from a Michigan real estate developer Combemale had barely heard of. He was A. Alfred Taubman, a legend in his own midwestern state and in California, where he had masterminded the biggest land deal, according to the press, since the Lousiana Purchase. Combemale had heard only good things about Taubman and he sounded like the man he was looking for. He was one of the richest people in America, worth by conservative calculation $500 million, most of the money having come from the sale of his holdings in the Southern California Irvine Ranch, an 80,000-acre parcel of prime Orange County turf running from the coastline to the mountains thirty miles south of Los Angeles. He was also an art collector and a member of several museum boards, including the Whitney Museum of American Art on Madison Avenue in New York and the Archives of American Art, headquartered in Washington, D.C.

Taubman was an empire builder and Sotheby's fit into his scheme. As a retailing wizard who specialized in luxury shopping centers in plush suburbs across America, he understood top-drawer marketing better than nearly anyone else. The year before, had anyone wanted proof that Sotheby's was part of Taubman's grand scheme, an official of the Taubman Company was quoted as saying in a magazine article that an outlet of Sotheby's would be a "possibility" in the Stamford Mall, a deluxe shopping extravaganza in Stamford, Connecticut, on the suburban gold coast less than forty miles northeast of midtown Manhattan, a few miles from John Marion's Federal-style farmhouse in suburban Darien.

With Taubman's kind of money, he could buy whatever he wanted. And he often did. During his brief period in bachelordom, following his divorce from his first wife and childhood sweetheart, Reva, Taubman was seen on the arm of such well-known bachelorettes as Zsa Zsa Gabor, and he was noted for his generosity and for his flamboyant displays when entertaining. He had recently married Judy Mazor Rounick, a beautiful blonde and former Miss Israel. Judy had worked behind the front counter at Christie's in New York, handing out catalogs and greeting rich clients. Although it was implicit, it was normally unspoken: Judy, whose first marriage had ended in divorce and a settlement she found less than satisfactory, was not unhappy to be working among Christie's stock of eligible millionaires. And she said so, on more than one occasion, in a breathy Eastern Mediterranean accent that left few wondering whether she would succeed. "Oh, is terrible being divorced," she confided to one of the greeters. "My mother had to buy my mink coat this season." Taubman, so the story goes, first laid eyes on his future second wife when she was spotting bidders in the salesroom, perched imperiously on a stool she had brought into the salesroom "because I don't like to stand." All of the other spotters stood, but not Judy.

Combemale also knew that Taubman was close to Henry Ford II, the scion of the car family and one of the most visible art collectors in the world; as well as Baron Hans Heinrich Thyssen-Bornemisza, the nephew of Fritz Thyssen, the man who financed the Third Reich. Even though Hitler later betrayed him, the Thyssen name has been long linked with the money behind the most notorious debacle in modern times. Heinie Thyssen, as the five-times-married baron is known to his good friends, has the largest private collection of art in the world, aside from the Queen of England. With friends like this, Combemale figured, it wouldn't matter that Taubman was barely known in New York and London, nor that he was Jewish.

So he was surprised when the call came in from the Taubman Company headquarters on West Big Beaver Road in Troy, Michigan. Taubman had looked over the proposal for the sale of Sotheby's. Try as he might, he could not figure out how a firm worth not more than $20 million in assets could command a $100 million price tag. His main interest, he told Combemale, was in the real estate, and there was precious little real estate, most of the Sotheby's offices being leased. He understood that the name alone was worth something, but he did not think he could go along with the scheme. His heart told him yes, Combemale inferred, but his brain was saying no.

As vast and seemingly diverse as the Taubman Company operation was then, it was still primarily a real estate development and construction company, and Taubman was wise enough to recognize that Sotheby's was a whole new game for him. He recognized that ownership of Sotheby's would bring him new— and much sought-after—cachet, and naturally would please Judy, who had been known to say that "auctions, you know, are in my blood." But he was not able to see Sotheby's as the banking operation Cogan and Swid had envisioned for the future of the art market. And Combemale, for all his energy and charm, was not prepared to present Sotheby's in such futuristic terms.

Sotheby's, Combemale soon recognized, was a tough firm to sell. The directors were already saying they would talk with *anyone* else to avoid talking with Cogan and Swid once more. The firm was being presented on a silver platter—an ornate antique silver platter—and no one wanted even to taste what was being offered. What Sotheby's thought it wanted was a union with a large corporation, preferably British, but that would not matter very much. Combemale thought he had found that corporation.

Over several lunches at Le Cirque, the pink midtown restaurant favored by the demimonde of New York society, Combemale met with American Express's Sanford Weill.

Weill was willing to renew talks between the two firms for a number of reasons, it seems, not the least of which had to do with his old business partner Marshall Cogan. With Cogan willing to go for the finish with Sotheby's, Weill felt compelled to look one more time at the place he had said was plagued by "all this English upper-class stuff." Weill is not the art aficionado Cogan, Swid, or Taubman is, but that did not seem to dampen his interest in the place, at least in February 1983.

So it was that Bernard Combemale dialed the London number of Lazard Brothers, the banking house, early one cold and blustery morning with the dark park looming ominously outside his library window at 960 Fifth Avenue. He was calling

Marcus Agius, a handsome young English banker he had met in the country at the home of Agius's Rothschild in-laws. Sotheby's being an English-run company traded in London, he would need an English banker, and Agius was his first choice.

"Allo! Marcus! Zis is Bernard, Bernard Combemale. How are you?"

Laughter.

"Yes, yes, very well. Yes, Pam is very well, sank you."

Agius had not heard from Combemale since the old days in Monaco, and he was naturally eager to find out how he had done in the meanwhile. The English, being more hidebound, find it difficult to understand the forgiving nature of most Americans and the way the comeback works.

"What can I do for you, Bernard?" Agius was eager to move away from the small talk Bernard so loved to indulge in.

"Well, you see, I am working on zis Sussebee's deal over here, and I have a few clients lined up I want you to work wiz."

"Who?"

"Well, zere is Alfred Taubman, zee big real estate developer from Michigan. And zen zere is Sandy Weill, zee American Express man. I sink Sussebee's will do anysing to avoid a take-over by Cogan and Swid."

Pause.

"Well, I think I can help you. Send me what you have on them. Send me what you have on the Sotheby's deal. And let me know as soon as you want me to start buying shares in Sotheby's for them."

"Zis is great, Marcus. I knew we could work well togezzer. Zis is great. I'll send you zee material by express mail."

Pause.

"Good-bye."

Agius was intrigued by the Sotheby's deal. He had naturally heard about the problems the firm had found with Cogan and Swid. And he was eager to find out more about why Sotheby's felt that a union between the two would be a disaster— for more reasons than the obvious. Lazard Brothers is owned by S. Pearson, the British conglomerate that also owns, among other properties, Madame Tussaud's, the waxworks. Pearson has been among the few British firms rumored as a candidate for Sotheby's hand in the current courtship. Sotheby's would become one of Agius's main projects in the months to follow. Little could Combemale have known how important his phone call to Agius would become to the future of Sotheby's.

TEN

THE next meeting of the board of directors of Sotheby Parke Bernet, p.l.c., was anything but civilized. There were no heart-shaped cookies or pretty pictures. The secret closed meeting, held in the International Thomson headquarters on March 11, 1983, included only the key directors of the international art auction house.

Jesse Wolff, the otherwise mild-mannered American lawyer who normally puffed on his pipe throughout such meetings, set the tone at the beginning. "If we have to play a rough American game with these two fellows," he said, "we will!"

The ten directors looked at each other with nods of approval. Like soldiers about to march to the front, the various board members had forgotten their differences. For more than an hour the closed-door meeting continued along these lines. Gordon Brunton mentioned the "blot" on Cogan's trading record that he had discovered. Even though it was no secret that Cogan had taken a voluntary suspension from trading in stocks in the United States, the news had not reached London until a few weeks before the meeting. The irony is that Brunton would not use this "blot" to full advantage as ammunition against the two Americans. Instead, the campaign against Cogan and Swid would quickly assume more personal attacks on the character of the two unwanted suitors. One of the directors who found the tone of the March 11 meeting unsavory, later said that Brunton did most of the talking and that what he talked about was not something he would like to repeat, although it was "decidedly hateful." Cogan and Swid, it seems, represented a bigger threat to Brunton than the loss of Sotheby's.

Backed by Wolff, who saw his two fellow Americans as members of the young and restless breed of Wall Street "sharpies" out for the quick kill, Brunton unleashed his fury. By the end of the meeting, Marion, Lally, Thompson, and most of all Llewellyn—all of the key directors—were fired by his emotional directive: Stop the two Americans at all costs.

For Wolff, the crusade against his fellow Jews and Americans must have involved mixed motives. On the one hand, he should have welcomed them—as they had hoped he would when they initially approached Sotheby's via his office. On the other hand, Cogan's trading record might jeopardize the future relations of Sotheby's with the SEC. He had a bad feeling about the two Americans. "As far as I can see, they did everything the wrong way," he later said. "If they wanted to talk to me, they should have called me on the phone, not worked through an intermediary. If they wanted to take the place over, they should have done so sooner than later."

The closed-door meeting had been called for precisely that reason. Cogan and Swid, the week before, had announced through a meeting in New York that they were prepared to make a bid for Sotheby's "sooner than later, within weeks rather than months." The meeting was held in the midtown offices of Goldman Sachs, the New York merchant bank Sotheby's had worked through over the years. As Sotheby's official spokesperson in America, the Goldman Sachs representative had told the two Americans that their bid would not be welcome and to brace themselves for a fight. Up until this point, Sotheby's had believed it could merely shoo the two away, like a horse's tail taking care of flies.

Cogan and Swid did not want to fight for Sotheby's. An

unwanted take-over bid runs the risk of all sorts of opposition in Britain, as Seelig, their banker at Morgan Grenfell, had warned them. To this end, they asked for a meeting with the senior "working" experts, as they defined the roles of two of the directors: Julian Thompson, the mild-mannered Chinese Art expert, and John Marion, the president of the U.S. arm of the firm. Brunton's London meeting was called to work up a response to their request, and within less than twenty-four hours Cogan and Swid learned what Sotheby's thought of their latest overture.

This was revealed in the press in various "leaked" accounts of what went on during the closed-door meeting. There was no official announcement of the minutes of the meeting, which was termed an "unannounced special" meeting in one account and, in another, "a regular monthly board meeting." "Sources" told *The New York Times* that the board had voted to fight the take-over attempt by GFI/Knoll. Another report quoted a source as saying that S. G. Warburg, Sotheby's English banker, had been directed to go on the defensive in the event of a bid from the two Americans. The seriousness of a prospective GFI/Knoll bid was confirmed by two revelations: one, that three banks—Citibank, Crocker National Bank, and Philadelphia National Bank—had agreed to back the unwanted suitors; two, of the shadow board Cogan and Swid had begun to set up with the help of Lord Harlech.

This was Sotheby's first counterattack in the battle that would last through the spring, and Cogan and Swid responded incredulously. Cogan, speaking from his penthouse office to *The New York Times*, confirmed that he had a "relationship" with Harlech, but pointed out that he and Swid had not decided whether to make a bid for the firm. Andrew Baer, the GFI/Knoll spokesperson, took up the offensive from Cogan. Speaking from his offices at Kekst and Company, the high-powered public relations outfit, Baer said that his clients were "disappointed" by the Sotheby's board's action in leaking their intentions through the media. "We had hoped this board would be a bit more open-minded," Baer said, "and that we could have proceeded in a professional and constructive manner."

Brunton told another paper that he could not disclose why he thought a bid would be imminent, but that Cogan and Swid had persisted in their request for a meeting with senior staff and working experts. "I can say that almost all of the twenty or thirty staff concerned said that they did not wish to meet them," Brunton said of the Cogan and Swid request. The staff Brunton was referring to was primarily the close-knit group of directors who felt that their jobs would be threatened by a Cogan and Swid take-over, and other loyal sycophants, of whom there were, to be sure, quite a number.

The staff will all walk is one of the oldest ploys in the annals of fending off take-overs. Had Brunton bothered to recall the reaction of the staff of *The Times* of London to the merger he arranged with Rupert Murdoch, he would have realized how silly such a declaration sounds. Some of them did leave; most found the job market for reporters and editors offered them few options, and in the end they remained at the paper in spite of their original misgivings. Brunton had denounced the staff for saying it would walk. Now, in a grand show of turnabout, he was taking the side of the staff.

For the most part, the staff had no idea who Cogan and Swid were, although many of them knew the name Harlech. Whether or not their association with Harlech helped or hurt the two Americans' bid is merely a topic for speculation. Cogan said he liked Harlech because he was a "maverick, like us." Llewellyn pointed out that Harlech was not only a maverick but, in Llewellyn's opinion, "persona non grata. I mean really," he said in an exasperated and arch tone, "Harlech! The lord for hire has agreed to be employed by our felt merchants."

The campaign to discredit the two Americans was begun in earnest that very week. Brunton issued a directive, according to many of the staff members, not to speak to the two Americans, although he denies having done so. Some began referring to the unwanted suitors as "bubble and squeak." Bubble and squeak is a traditional English dish consisting of potatoes and cabbage, named for the sound those vegetables make when fried. And in Cockney rhyming slang, *bubble and squeak* has several meanings, including "a Greek" and "to speak," particularly in the sense of informing on one's partners in crime.

Bubble and squeak was their code name, and the objective was to eliminate them. Within days a group of steadfast employees, led by Richard Camber, a senior expert in charge of decorative arts, approached Brunton with a proposal. They would write a letter to the two Americans, threatening to quit in the event that their take-over succeeded. Brunton liked the idea very much indeed and he rewarded Camber with a big smile, which he had not shown him before. Camber felt close to Brunton, he later said, because his wife is somehow related to Lord Thomson, and he apparently wanted to grow even closer.

The letter proved to be more troublesome than Camber thought it would be. He and Brunton had agreed that it would carry more weight with the signatures of all the employees on both sides of the Atlantic and in Europe. But, while Camber would argue the case against Cogan and Swid in London, there was no one in New York or in Europe to do so—at least not at first. Within days everyone had heard about the letter and that it was in effect a letter of resignation, signed en masse, by the entire staff. Which it was, in its original form. For Camber had written that the staff "would seek alternative employment" in the event of a take-over by the two Americans.

In the various unofficial meetings that took place in the Bond Street salesroom, Camber pushed his point with the determination of a politician running for office. Cogan and Swid, he implied, were dangerous Americans, and it did not take long for the staff members to form a mental image of the types of Americans they particularly did not like. Within a few days Camber had collected more than fifty signatures for his letter. Brunton was pleased, but he insisted that signatures come from America as well.

America was another matter. For here a campaign could not be mounted against Cogan and Swid on the basis of their nationality. The staff in America had mostly mixed emotions about the possibility of the take-over. Even John Marion had no great affection for the British management. For Jim Lally, however, the Cogan and Swid matter was a topic he could get worked up over.

As a fellow Harvard alumnus, Lally had never really liked Cogan, Cogan maintained: "And if there was anyone I would rather not have seen [at Sotheby's], he would have been near the top of the list." Lally and Wooley organized a secret meeting of their own in Wooley's Fifth Avenue apartment during the week of March 20.

There, to the accompaniment of the tweets of an indoor aviary that must have made conversation fairly difficult, the senior staff of the U.S. branch met to discuss the letter, and how they could persuade their colleagues to sign it. They decided to change the wording of the letter, from "would seek alternative employment" to "would consider alternative employment." After all, no one wants to sign a resignation letter without truly wishing to resign.

The next day at a meeting of the general staff on York Avenue, the letter was presented and questions were answered by Marion and Lally. Hermine Chivian-Cobb, the modern-drawings specialist who has since left to set up her own business, asked Marion why they should sign the letter and why Cogan and Swid were such bad people. Neither of her questions was answered. As a result there was much grumbling afterward.

The letter was finally sent to the press on April 3, by special hand delivery, from Gordon Brunton's office. It was written on International Thomson letterhead and addressed to Roger Seelig, the two Americans' banker at Morgan Grenfell. The following day the letter appeared in the British papers, although more than a few of them noted that GFI/Knoll had increased its stake in Sotheby's in spite of the missive. Other reports pointed out that Sotheby's had seriously risked future business by sending out such a letter. In a business like Sotheby's, where consignments, the backbone of the operation, are received several months before sale, the prospect of the staff's walking out would destroy confidence: The consignors could simply sell through Christie's until the matter had been settled.

In less enlightened London circles, the names Cogan and

Swid were soon standard objects of derision, as though the two marauders from the West had robbed a bank, or worse. This should come as no surprise to anyone familiar with English ways. "The thing about these two," one English banker explained, "is that no one knows them."

"Are they rich?" a socialite familiar with the case asked incredulously. "Not rich enough, I suspect. We like anyone rich, even if they are Americans." Poor Lord Harlech, the "lord for hire," had to endure many such barbed remarks that spring.

"Dear David," intoned a lady of some standing in the London art world, walking up to Harlech at a fancy gathering in Belgravia. "Have you heard the news about Sotheby's?"

"What news?" he asked, expecting to hear yet another story about Sotheby's debacle. The lady being a lady and Harlech being a lord made no difference when they spoke to each other. He was David as far as she was concerned.

"The place is being taken over by these two awful Americans."

"Oh, well, I have met them. You must mean Cogan and Swid."

"Precisely. Is that how you pronounce their names? I thought it was CAH-gun."

"Yes, well, they are really not so bad. Really. I've met them."

"No, no, David, you must have them mixed up with some other Americans you've met. I know you know quite a few Americans."

"Really, they are not so bad."

"David, you're wrong. I have heard that they are the *worst* sort of Americans. The worst."

Nothing could be worse than the worst sort of Americans. Even Australians were better. Canadians, much better. Perhaps South Africans were worse, but that was another matter altogether. Fortunately for the two worst sort of Americans, the stock market responded democratically to their unofficial bid for shares in Sotheby's. Even as the talk in Belgravia turned for the most part against them, the talk in the City awarded them a larger and larger share in Sotheby's. Sooner than later they would be forced to make an active bid for Sotheby's. It seemed there was nothing any talk could do to prevent the "felt merchants from New Jersey" from buying in.

ELEVEN

HIGH in their penthouse suite above London, Cogan and Swid mapped out their strategy. Mere insults could not deter them; the self-styled mavericks had almost come to expect rough treatment.

With their lawyer, Stanley Berwin, and financial advisers Susan Lipton and Roger Seelig, they looked to the future. The future looked more and more like a place where Cogan and Swid would run Sotheby's. Not that they really wanted to do so, at least to hear them talk about it. "They antagonized us, and left us with little choice in the matter. It was a matter of honor in the end. We were forced to make the bid."

If only, they thought, they could divide the board members and persuade at least a few of them to agree to a union of parts rather than a take-over battle. It was one thing to buy into Sotheby's, quite another to threaten to fire belted earls. This is what Seelig and Berwin, two Britishers familiar with the almost medieval system of English government, warned the two Americans about. The odds in favor of a successful Anglo-American merger between the two teams would be much better if at least a few of Sotheby's board members could be convinced that this was in their best interests.

Swid had already spoken with Peter Wilson about the matter over the phone. Wilson, too, was looking to the future, and in his case the future was the Gould sale-of-the-century coming up, and other sales from which he could draw a handsome commission. Being, if nothing else, a well-groomed political animal, Wilson knew he had to cover all bases. While he did not commit himself to the two Americans wholeheartedly, he did intimate in a phone conversation from Château de Clavary that he would work with Cogan and Swid in the event of a take-over. "I will do nothing to jeopardize the future of Sotheby's," he said. "The firm itself means more to me than any alliances I may have."

Then the silver department paid a call at the Park Lane Hotel. Led by Richard Came, the affable and competent working expert in charge of sales of antique silver, they listened to Cogan and Swid offer them profit sharing in their department. Fearful of being caught in this act of outright sedition, Came would later deny he had made a visit to the enemy camp, but he did. And he left convinced that these fellows were "not so bad at all," as Lord Harlech had tried to tell her ladyship.

Came was fed up with the present management of Sotheby's, and he was not alone. As a Wilson man, he did not understand what Brunton or Llewellyn was trying to do with the company. "They led us around," he said, "by rings in our noses. It really made me angry after a while. No one could make decisions. There was absolutely no decision making."

Another senior working expert echoed Came's complaints. He said the numerous and aimless meetings literally drove him to distraction. At one such, for more than two hours a committee of people discussed the catalog format, which had traditionally varied from department to department, from London to New York to Monte Carlo. To save money, as part of the cost-cutting scheme instituted by Brunton, it was decided that the catalogs should all be the same size and format so that paper could be ordered in larger quantities. The problem was that all of them wanted to retain the formats they had already been using. "It was a nightmare, like something out of a theater of the absurd," the expert said.

Then there was the round-table meeting. In New York, back at the York Avenue boondoggle, a meeting was held to discuss the board dining room, which remained unfinished and unopened for the first year or so. The meeting was called to discuss the table, and what kind of table it should be. According to one who was present, the directors discussed for hours the relative merits of round, square, and rectangular tables. "It was finally decided," he said in exasperated tones, "that the meeting should be tabled! This was after hours of talk, or what seemed like hours. The problem I think was that no one wanted a rectangular table, because no one could decide who should sit at the head of the table during meetings. I mean there were at least four people who all thought they were the chief operating officers."

A glance at the roster of directors and titles would have confirmed this observation. Even the head of corporate communications, an executive who should know such things, could not unravel the Byzantine twistings of Sotheby's upper management. At a meeting in the spring of 1983, Elizabeth Robbins attempted to draw a chart showing the chain of command through at least five layers of personnel. At the top of the chart were the names of Gordon Brunton, as chief non-executive officer, and Graham Llewellyn, as chief executive officer. Then the boxes and lines began to get so confused as one name followed another, overlapping at some points, crisscrossing at others, that the chart finally ran off the side of the page. Looking down at the mess of names and boxes and arrows, she threw up her hands, glanced around the room nervously, and said, "Well, let's talk about something else. You get the picture."

Cogan and Swid were getting the picture too. Eventually, they hoped, some of Sotheby's voting officials would come over to their side and then the whole thing would be easier for them. Looking carefully at a chart of their own making, they decided to ask yet again for a meeting, this time with John Marion, Julian Thompson, president of the London operation, and Peter Wilson. The one glaring omission in the GFI/Knoll chart was

Graham Llewellyn. As the chief executive officer and working head of the jewelry department, he should have been included, but Cogan and Swid had already decided, from their research, that Llewellyn was not an important player in their plans for Sotheby's.

Sotheby's agreed to the meeting with one condition: James Lally should come along. Cogan and Swid agreed, though Cogan wished they could have said no. At least Sotheby's had agreed to meet with them again. Little did they know why.

Sotheby's had not been sitting on its hands. The directors continued to beat the bushes in search of someone, anyone, more acceptable than the two Americans. The search took the fifteenth earl of Westmorland on a plane trip to the Bahamas one fine early spring weekend for a secret meeting with a man who would soon be hailed as Sotheby's savior.

Cogan and Swid had no idea who that might be. They fully expected Sanford Weill, Cogan's former partner. Now Cogan was not about to let Weill take Sotheby's away from him. "Sandy Weill knows as much about art as that duck over there," he said, "and I don't want him to get into Sotheby's because he wouldn't know what to do with it." Cogan claims he threatened to expose Weill in the press as someone who could not mastermind "his way out of a paper bag," and as a result, Weill backed down. Combemale, however, maintains that he introduced Weill to Brunton, but the two men could not agree on a price for Sotheby's. Also pertinent, perhaps, is the fact that Weill's star was fading at Amex and he would soon depart the firm to set up his own business.

The meeting in the Bahamas was hosted by an old friend of Westmorland's and of Sotheby's: David Metcalfe. His interest in the auction house was as much business as social. Metcalfe is one of those people who cut a wide swath across international society on several continents. Based in the Bahamas, where he was raised, he travels frequently: New York, London, Monte Carlo, Geneva, Zurich, and anywhere else the rich and famous might be found. He looks tall and drawn (albeit suntanned) in the English aristocratic manner. His father, Major Edward Dudley (Fruitie) Metcalfe, was aide-de-camp to

the Duke of Windsor and settled in the Bahamas with the abdicated king and the former Mrs. Simpson during the Second
World War, a period when gambling was being introduced to
the economy there.

David Metcalfe was just the sort of person who could help
Sotheby's out. And he was just the sort of person David Westmorland would trust to do the job correctly, and locate someone out there in the world of big money and fancy art who would
appeal more to Sotheby's way of doing business. By the time
Sotheby's board walked into the next meeting with the two
Americans, it was prepared to fight to the finish, confident that
the Bahamas connection would pay off.

The meeting requested by Cogan and Swid was set for April
1983 in the Sotheby's Chippendale boardroom on New Bond
Street in London. The two "felt fellows" could not help but notice a few details Sotheby's brought into play this time. The most
important of these were the time and place of the gathering:
midafternoon on a Sunday, the quietest time of the week in
Sotheby's and along New Bond Street, the auction house being
closed to the public like most of its chic neighbors—Yves St.
Laurent, Gucci, Claude Montana. And how they got there was
somewhat out of the ordinary. "They let us in by the *back* door,"
Cogan would later exclaim.

Llewellyn claims it was not so unusual to enter through the
back—shipping and delivery—door on Sundays. The back door
leads directly up to the second-floor boardroom, whereas to get
to the boardroom from the front door on New Bond means dis-
connecting a series of burglar alarms set up throughout the maze
of nineteenth-century hallways and chambers that make up the
main salesroom. Nor does Llewellyn feel it was so unusual that
the rectangular table was so cramped. But Cogan, who hates
facing walls or confined spaces, felt dizzy with claustrophobia.

"They brought their whole crew," Llewellyn says disdainfully. "Their whole crew of sharpies arrived in a caravan of
long black hired automobiles. Daimlers, I believe."

The "crew of sharpies" included Cogan and Swid's advisers Roger Seelig, Philip Evans from Morgan Grenfell, Stanley
Berwin, a famous London barrister, and Marty and Susan Lip-

ton, an American couple who specialize in take-over battles. The day was raw and dim; the salesroom's rear hallways dark, cold, and dirty. They had arrived fully prepared for whatever might be hurled their way, but the circumstances looked bad before they had even entered the boardroom. Once inside, their suspicions were only reinforced.

At the first meeting pleasantries had been exchanged and hands shaken around the table; this time Brunton merely stood up from his seat and motioned for them to sit down. The battle lines were clearly drawn. Sotheby's directors sat on one side of the table, "practically in each other's laps," according to Cogan; the GFI/Knoll crew occupied the other side, facing the directors. There were cut-crystal decanters filled with water in between. But before anyone could think of taking a drink, Brunton began his introductory comments. Echoing his first speech to the two Americans about having "made a mistake," he continued to point out that there was "no synergy" between Sotheby's and GFI/Knoll, again saying, "You are in *manufacturing*" (punctuated with a grimace); "we are a prestigious auction house."

Brunton then unharnessed a vituperative fury. He blamed the two Americans for Sotheby's poor figures, which continued to slump downward. He said their attack on Sotheby's had caused the house to lose consignments, and he even had a very good and dear-to-his-heart example. "*Lord* Astor," he said deferentially, "has personally called me to express his deep misgivings about you." Should they succeed in their quest for the firm, Brunton reported that Astor had told him over the phone, "I will have no choice but to remove my armor suits from Sotheby's, and sell through Christie's." Brunton hammered his point home with such conviction that it sounded as if all of London were recoiling at the mention of the two men.

Julian Thompson took over where Brunton left off. Unlike Brunton, who tended to raise his voice and stare down his nose menacingly, Thompson was calmer in manner but colder. White with pain, having not fully recuperated from multiple injuries sustained in a car crash the previous fall, the Chinese art scholar gave the reasons why he would not work with the two. He said he thought they would "exploit" the "good" name of Sotheby's for their own "personal profit." His clients, he said, were also repelled by them, as Astor had been. His colleagues and assistants would not work with them either. Then, looking straight across the table to where Cogan and Swid were sitting, he stated the bottom line: "You are simply not our kind," he said, deliberately and calmly, and then added after a brief pause, "of Americans."

The angel of silence passed over the room. No one spoke. No one even looked at anyone else. Cogan could hear only a buzz in his inner ear as the other directors began their speeches. He cannot remember much of what Sotheby's "kind of Americans," Lally and Marion, had to say. Marion kept his comments brief. Lally, it seems to Cogan, echoed Thompson's remarks, not only in content but in accent and pronunciation. "They treated us like pariahs," Cogan would later say, over and over.

The two Americans proceeded to meet in private, in the adjacent kitchen, with the "working" directors, as Marion, Lally, Thompson, and Wilson had been designated by the suitors. There, under the glare of a bright fluorescent fixture, with the pungent vegetal aroma characteristic of many British kitchens filling the air, Cogan and Swid made their final plea. The four working directors listened attentively as they outlined what they thought Sotheby's should do to "restore profitability and increase market share." There was more talk about profit-sharing incentives to motivate the working experts to become more aggressive. This made some sense to all of them: Working experts often bring home as little as $20,000 for producing sales that bring in millions. But they were not willing to concede the company line, as it had been clearly set out in the preceding spectacle. None of them, that is, except Wilson.

Cogan and Swid were spellbound as the tall and aristocratic chairman emeritus rose from his kitchen chair and made a little speech. In a deeply coded message that could be taken either way, characteristic of the master rhetorician and former spy, Wilson more or less embraced the unwanted suitors. He reiterated that he had only the future of the firm in mind and that no one should do anything to jeopardize that future, which had already been damaged. He said he agreed with Cogan and Swid's suggestions, but that the decision was not his alone. Thompson, Marion, and Lally looked somewhat surprised by his outpouring, but no one who knew Wilson could have been truly surprised.

As the kitchen meeting disbanded and the seven made their way back into the main boardroom, Wilson approached Cogan and gave him another message. "I have not spoken with Brunton," he said softly, "in more than six months."

Back outside in the raw April weather, Cogan decided to go for a walk alone in the damp gloom that had descended over London. Despite the cryptic encouragement from Wilson, Cogan was deeply depressed by the tone of the meeting. After the way he and Swid had attacked the management of Sotheby's he can hardly have expected them to embrace him. Still, he felt more than ever that anti-Semitism was responsible for the nastiness of their response.

TWELVE

COGAN and Swid were through playing nice. The day after the meeting, a twelve-page official offering document was rushed from Morgan Grenfell to the proper channels in the City and to the press. The two Americans, under the GFI/Knoll banner, would offer shareholders nearly $7 per share (520 pence) for the remaining stock in Sotheby Parke Bernet & Company, p.l.c. The Americans were prepared to fight to the finish. Their shadow board and high-priced specialists were geared for action. Their financing had come through, awaiting only their nod for the money to be released to shareholders. With just six weeks to act upon the offer, the time limit set by GFI, shareholders had little time to think twice about this more than attractive bid.

For those who had not followed Sotheby's plight closely, the reaction of the troubled firm seemed more than emotional; it seemed hysterical. And well it might have been, with no chance of a profit or a dividend to shareholders this year, and a couple of Americans offering investors nearly double what their shares had been worth before the bidding battle started with the first GFI/Knoll purchase the previous fall. Shares that had been worth only slightly more than $3 (250 pence) each were now swelled with newfound value, even though the performance of the firm "could not justify the increase," according to the offering document.

The GFI/Knoll bid, according to the press release issued through Warburg's, was "wholly unwelcome." Llewellyn, who had been appointed official spokesman for Sotheby's, said they would "use every weapon at their command," and then embroidered on the official line. The bid, he said, was "wholly unwelcome," because these two Americans were "wholly unacceptable." His only explanation of what he meant was: "They're just the wrong kind of people." Presumably most people would read between the lines, at least the people that counted, notably the shareholders.

Phone calls poured into the salesroom, and Llewellyn had only a few minutes to grab a quick lunch with Jesse Wolff. The excitement had fired his blood with new enthusiasm. He was at the helm of a sinking ship and, like a good captain, going to fight until the mast dropped into the sea. On their way back up the warren of stairs and hallways to one of the cell-like rooms he called an office, Llewellyn seemed particularly agitated and Wolff noticed this with concern. "Hold on, Graham," Wolff said. "This is really not that bad. You're not going to blow your brains out over this." Little did Wolff know how far gone Llewellyn was.

The two men settled into Llewellyn's cozy office for a brief talk when the phone interrupted them. It was Geraldine Norman, the salesroom correspondent for *The Times* of London. Llewellyn took the call, and chatted with her for several minutes, giving her the standard answers to the standard questions. Then he laughed for a brief spell, collected his thoughts, and spoke into the phone slowly and teasingly: "What will I do if they succeed with their bid?" he repeated Norman's question. "I'll tell you what I'll do. I'll blow my brains out—that's what I'll do."

A look of deep concern clouded Wolff's otherwise calm face. "You shouldn't have said that, Graham," Wolff pointed out, suggesting that he call Norman back immediately. It was too late.

Norman, like any good journalist knowing a good story, had rushed the quote into print.

The Take-over Panel, a government watchdog agency that monitors take-over bids involving British companies, stepped in the following day. John Hignett, the head of the panel, had read Llewellyn's remark in the morning's *Times*. This was not good, and strong measures were needed immediately. Llewellyn would be censured publicly. The motion carried no fine or punishment, only the sting of public embarrassment, which is much greater in the small and fastidious world of London business than it might seem to Americans. "It is extremely important," Hignett told Warburg's Hugh Stevenson over the phone, "for people to say precisely what they mean during a take-over. I don't believe Llewellyn meant what he said at all. For that reason, I must censure him immediately."

No one at Sotheby's was pleased with Llewellyn's censure, but no one made an issue of the matter. Llewellyn's high-strung state was shared by most of the other directors, including Brunton, and far be it from them to make an issue of shared hysteria. In a perverse way, Sotheby's had hammered home its point to its target audience: British institutions and shareholders, representing some 42 percent of its investors. Surely they wouldn't sell out to the two Americans—or would they? By the end of the week, Cogan and Swid had boosted their share by 6 percent, bringing their total to 20 percent plus, proving they would. Someone was selling, and others were also buying. The share price jumped quickly to 535 pence each, 15 pence above the GFI/Knoll offer. This was a natural market reaction to a formal bid. Arbitrageurs, hoping to make a quick dollar (or pound) by speculating in shares of the firm, were among the other buyers. The overall American holdings in the stock climbed rapidly; and by Friday, the unofficial tally put the American share at 50 percent. All Cogan and Swid needed to declare victory would be 50 percent of the shares plus one, under British take-over law.

But London, they soon learned, works differently from New York. The cluster of once-small villages that make up the greater London area often seems hopelessly confusing, but the town works remarkably well at times. Fortified by strong cups of tea, rejuvenated by more pastoral housing conditions, unhindered by the long lunch hours that make business in New York a split affair—all these combine to make the town run more smoothly than almost any in the world. Not to mention the proximities of London, which contrast with New York, where Wall Street is five miles from the Park Avenue world headquarters of the Fortune 500 ilk—an often impossibly congested five miles at that. Washington and the government is even farther away, forty minutes by air. In London, Whitehall, the City, and the West End corporate headquarters are all within a walk, a short drive, or a speedy underground train ride of each other. With seven daily newspapers, five of which carry varying degrees of authority, London also has a better communications system, even though the phones remain fairly bad by comparison with New York's.

News travels faster there, and so it was no surprise to anyone that by Thursday, Sotheby's board had pushed a member of Parliament into action to help repel the unwanted suitors. The motion was "put forward," in the parlance of the seven-hundred-year-old governing body, by John Ryman, Labour representative to the House of Commons from Blyth, Northumberland. As a historic-preservation advocate, Ryman was an MP who could be counted on to help save Sotheby's. In his motion Ryman argued that such an "essentially British institution as Sotheby's should not be swallowed by two rich Americans who were artistically and intellectually unacceptable." Note the word *unacceptable* surfacing again. Note too that Ryman described them as rich, whereas Brunton claimed they could not afford Sotheby's. It is also interesting that he attacked their standing artistically and intellectually, presumably without having discussed German Expressionist art or Kierkegaard with the two. Ryman called for direct government intervention, seeking a referral of the bid to the Monopolies and Mergers Commission through the office of Peter Rees in the Department of Trade.

This is not as unusual as it might seem. Seeking a referral to the Monopolies and Mergers Commission is the first thing anyone does in the case of an unwelcome take-over attempt. Rees

answered that he would look into the matter and decide whether
to refer the bid to the commission, a step which would take up
to six months and possibly thwart the GFI/Knoll attempt.

But, arguing that a sale to two Americans would create a
monopoly in the London art market was just not possible. The
London art market was already crowded with other auctioneers—Christie's and Phillips the most visible among the
group—willing to pick up the slack. "Normal competitive policy," Seelig explained carefully, "did not apply."

So Seelig told the two Americans that they should not worry
about the possibility of a referral. The Thatcher government,
up for reelection in June, had based its successful run on
Downing Street on several counts that would make intervention
unlikely. The government was about as pro-free trade and anti-
interventionist as any since Balfour's Edwardian regime. With
the Falklands victory under her cap and the first robust economy in nearly a decade, Thatcher would not want to do anything that could be used against her. The decision was hers or,
rather, that of one of her closest cabinet members, Lord Cockfield, the trade minister, a like-minded pro-free- and fair-trade
advocate.

There was always the off-chance of power-broking in the
tight web of London men's clubs and old school ties. Seelig and
Berwin, as relative outsiders in this web, were not about to leave
anything to chance. Since Cogan and Swid had been treated like
"pariahs" by Sotheby's board, the banker and lawyer mar-
shaled evidence to prove that they were, if not brahmins, then
very much *menshen*. They may not be *our class, dear*, but as
proved by the letters of recommendation Cogan and Swid received from such illustrious leaders as William Batten, chairman of the New York Stock Exchange, the Honorable Edward
Kennedy, U.S. senator from Massachusetts, and the dean of
Harvard College, they were well respected on their home turf.
These letters were sent, along with other pertinent details to back
up their case, to Sir Gordon Borrie, director of the Office of
Fair Trading. It was Borrie who would eventually decide whether
or not to refer the bid to the Monopolies Commission. Although
he could be overruled by Cockfield, the trade minister, direct

lobbying of the top ministers is frowned upon in Britain—one of those things that is simply not done.

Here is where Cogan and Swid could have benefited from being better connected socially. For, while direct lobbying is frowned upon, there is no reason a minister could not be buttonholed at a drinks party on Eaton Place or a dinner in Belgravia. Being socially connected, however, has never been a goal of the two Americans. "The thing about those two," said a leading New York party-planner, "is that they are all work, no play. They don't go out for pleasure. I never see them after ten P.M. If it's an official function, they work the room and go home."

As Geraldine Norman concluded in *The Times* on Friday, April 15, in her analysis of the lack of "synergy": "If only they were famous," Norman speculated, "and better connected, Sotheby's might be able to welcome them as collaborators in building the business. They would then have some 'synergy' with the millionaire collectors, jet setters and ruined aristocrats selling off their heirlooms who constitute the clientele."

Fortunately for the two parvenus, the press in Britain is not finely attuned to what is being said in Belgravia or on Eaton Square. Both Cogan and Swid were well received by all but the staunchly conservative *Daily Telegraph*, and even its coverage depended on who was reporting. In the *Financial Times*, the bulwark of British business decision making, Ian Hargreaves and Charles Batchelor wrote: "For men who have been practically accused of undermining the British way of life, Marshall S. Cogan and Stephen C. Swid are a remarkably mild-mannered duo."

Indeed, the press rallied to the defense of the mild-mannered duo. Sotheby's attacked Cogan for his run-in with the Securities and Exchange Commission. The *Daily Telegraph*, reporting on this blot on his trading record, concluded that it had been "scotched." Sotheby's accused the two Americans of plans to exploit the name of the firm through licensing it to cigarette manufacturers or through their own furniture firm. (Not that the idea was novel: In 1973, Wilson attempted to raise money by selling the name to Rothschild for an ill-fated up-scale cigarette; it failed, perhaps because people thought they were buying

a package of antique butts.) The *Financial Times* allowed the
two Americans the lead paragraph of a front-page story for their
rebuttal to the claim, burying the details of Cogan's brush with
the SEC in the thirteenth paragraph. As to the charge, the *Financial Times* concluded that it had been settled.

Every charge that issued from either New Bond Street or
Thomson headquarters was dismissed in the press as so much
hot air. While the mild-mannered duo charmed reporters from
their airy penthouse suite high above London, hotheaded Llewellyn continued to offend the same reporters with his patrician
airs. He issued proclamations like "They have never been to an
auction"—which was untrue. Then he would sum up his disdain for the two Americans by saying with a sniff, "These people are, after all, in the manufacturing business."

Over in Thomson headquarters, Brunton would point out
that the two Americans' financing would jeopardize the future
of the firm, as though this argument would dissuade shareholders from selling off. Whenever reporters would probe the nonexecutive chairman for more details about this financing, he
would segue into balance-sheet jargon about debt-equity ratio
and how Cogan and Swid would bring a dangerous one to Sotheby's.

The staff was nearly held under lock and key. All communication was handled through Brunton, Thompson, or Llewellyn. There was no communication out of New York, and the
press offices in both London and New York were blamed for
the poor response to Sotheby's case in the media. Finally,
Goldman Sachs, the New York investment house searching
frantically for a White Knight to rescue the besieged company,
brought in an outside press consultant to handle the more delicate communiqués. Of the 133 staff members who had signed
the missive to Cogan and Swid, more than a few began to wish
they hadn't.

And then one broke lose. Nabil Saida placed his call to
Geraldine Norman at *The Times* nearly a week into the official
battle. Saida, a world-renowned specialist in the field of oriental manuscripts, had had enough. "We are being led around
like sheep," he told Norman. "We are told we will be fired if

we talk to Cogan or Swid. We don't even know them or what they represent. How can we object to them if we cannot even meet them?" Saida later said that he did not care what the consequences of his seditious act would be; he was prepared to accept whatever punishment the directors had in store for him. Sotheby's, he said, "had become a living nightmare."

Saida arrived at work early on the morning of April 21 prepared to clean out his desk. For there on the front page of *The Times* were his name and complaint about being led around "like sheep"; the word *sheep* even appeared in the headline. He was ready for the calls from Llewellyn and Thompson when they came through. As he made his way across the maze of Sotheby's corridors and hallways, up the narrow red-carpeted stairway, on the way to their high-level offices, he took pride in what he had done. He noted happily that some of his colleagues smiled at him, while others even had the guts to approach him and say hello.

His worst fears were quickly laid to rest: Neither Thompson nor Llewellyn seemed visibly upset, and they reassured him that he would not lose his job for having spoken out. There was little they could have done: To fire him would only have vindicated his claim about their reign of terror. "They told me I shouldn't have done what I did," he said. "They said it had ruined their game plan and would cost the firm."

The game plan was hardly Llewellyn's or Thompson's creation. Warburg's, under the direction of Hugh Stevenson and stewardship of Gordon Brunton, had masterminded it: Fend off the marauders at any cost to image or credibility. Unfortunately for Warburg's, some of Sotheby's directors, notably Llewellyn, had taken the game too seriously and lost their heads.

There was more than childish bullying at play. Sotheby's unwanted suitors were Jews, and the word *unacceptable* and the phrase *not our kind of people* left a nasty taste in some quarters. There was—and still is—quite a bit of talk in private about the significance of Sotheby's attack on Cogan and Swid. Some have even said that, as a result, Goldman Sachs was instructed by Warburg's to find a Jew in America, presumably to avoid further talk of anti-Semitism. The New York office had in fact located a White Knight, and the savior had even gone as far as ordering stock for his account through Marcus Agius at Lazard Brothers.

But the White Knight needed time to mount his steed. Cogan and Swid, however, seemed invincible. The government was sympathetic to their plight, and would probably approve their bid. Sotheby's had not presented a logical defense. Not to mention the reaction of the shareholders. By April 22, barely a week into the formal bid, the two Americans were practically victorious, with more than 20—some said as much as 30—percent of Sotheby's stock on hand, and additional commitments for more than 50 percent. Some 80 percent of Sotheby's had drifted across the Atlantic. The place was in enemy hands.

THIRTEEN

LIKE Cogan and Swid, GJW Government Relations was asked to Sotheby's on a Sunday, and told to use the same back door off George Street. It wouldn't do for lobbyists to wander freely through the halls of "one of Britain's great institutions" during normal operating hours. Not that anyone would recognize the faces of Andrew Gifford, Jenny Jeger, or Wilf Weeks. Unless perhaps an Arab oil sheik dropped by to visit Nabil Saida, or a Liverpudlian record mogul to look at David Hockney drawings. For these were the usual clients of lobbyists like GJW, clients whose influence in the government and connections in the old-boy network were nil.

The irony of Sotheby's predicament had struck Gifford the moment he received the phone call from a somewhat addled Hugh Stevenson at Warburg's the preceding Thursday. Being an ironical sort of person—with long hair like a rock musician, a collection of "moduhn" art, and left-wing politics—Gifford relishes it when they come to him on a silver platter, as this one did. Was he familiar with the Sotheby's case? the voice on the other end squeaked through the receiver. (This was the day *The Times* had splashed Saida's indiscretion across the front page, and even the bag ladies in Piccadilly Circus, probably even the pigeons, knew of the Sotheby's case.) And could he help out with it?

Gifford and his two partners are practical people, ironies notwithstanding. The Sotheby's case was a valuable account. How valuable they would not say, but it was enough to make Gifford smile at the thought of the bill. It was also a rush job and not an easy one.

Although to some xenophobes in Belgravia and Eaton Square the two Americans were still the objects of schoolboy taunts, public opinion had all but turned in their favor. Sotheby's, the thinking went, had not behaved like gentlemen, and the newspapers, government, stock market, shareholders—even, so the story goes, Prime Minister Thatcher—had turned against the auction house, antique institution though it might be. "They have acted outrageously," one of the more sympathetic denizens of Eaton Square's party circuit said of the directors. "And they should be whipped!" he added, choosing a metaphor in keeping with the childish light in which the directors were perceived in many quarters.

Gifford did not need to be reminded of how badly things were going for Sotheby's. The desperation of the directors was written all over their faces, as he could see after a moment's glance around the conference table. Llewellyn, having taken the issue closest to heart, looked the worst: "Practically over the top," Gifford recalled, with an Englishism for *zonkers*. Brunton had a deep frown etched into his face, a distinctly English sort of frown that seems to hang down to the knees. Thompson looked white as a sheet and "pinched with pain." Only Wilson and Westmorland, who sported faint suntans acquired on their recent trip to the Bahamas and Palm Beach in search of White Knights in their winter sunning grounds, appeared remotely presentable.

The contrast was striking: Here were three young experts telling some of Britain's sage old figures how to conduct themselves. Perhaps it was the weather, which was once again, according to the upper right front corner of *The Times*, dim. Perhaps it was the English respect for expertise, which had of course allowed Sotheby's to call anyone with a passing knowledge of art an expert. Perhaps it was out of sheer desperation. Whatever the reason, as the dynamic trio of lobbyists began their presentation, the directors merely sat back, folded their hands in well-clothed laps, and listened attentively, like children.

Gifford wasted no time on niceties. Instead, he launched into the new game plan he and his colleagues had devised to save Sotheby's through a referral to the Monopolies and Mergers Commission. This was no easy matter. "There is no clear legal basis for the argument," Gifford concluded.

There was, however, a loophole. Under the Fair Trading Act of 1973, the Office of Fair Trading received power that goes beyond consideration of a monopoly. In deciding whether to refer a bid to the commission, the office may also consider what effect a change in hands would have on the public's confidence in the market; that is, whether the bid is in the public interest. The public-interest argument, while subjective and difficult to build, might go something like this: Allowing Sotheby's to pass into American hands was not in the public interest because it would jeopardize London's preeminent position in the international art market, a position it had nearly lost to New York anyway. London would lose jobs. London would lose tourist revenue from hotels and restaurants.

World-ranking scholars and experts, like the Chinese-art man Julian Thompson, would be out of work if the two Americans took over the company. Which leads us to part two of the GJW campaign to gain the sympathy of the government. There would be no more hand-wringing or unseemly gnashing of teeth in public. There would be no more personal attacks made on the unwanted suitors; no longer would they be billed as philistines who could not tell a Tintoretto from a *Playboy* pinup.

The public-interest defense was so useful. It would be dear to the heart of the Prime Minister, who clutches the public interest to her breast like a hen her chicks. Doubtless it would lead to a referral of the unwelcome bid.

"We will need new faces to lead the new campaign," Gifford said, looking around the room at the ravaged faces staring up at him, as though he were about to punish some of them—

which, in a way, he was. He looked down at his feet as he said who the new leaders would be. Thompson, because of his position in the Chinese art field, would be one of the holdovers. The other two would be Wilson and Westmorland. Between the two of them, the cousins had more connections in higher places than any other board members—practically more than all the others combined. They were, after all, the grandsons of Lord Ribblesdale, the keeper of Queen Victoria's buckhounds, and Westmorland was the fifteenth earl. Better yet, the two aristocrats had kept themselves more or less on the sidelines during the nastier rounds with the two Americans.

Brunton took the news with stony-faced resignation, like a good trooper. There was little point in his objecting to the new game plan. The old game plan had failed. Moreover, he could not claim the connections Wilson and Westmorland enjoyed: As a Canadian Tory who holds undying loyalty to the crown and the peerage, he respected those old-boy ties. The non-executive chairman and spokesman for the battle would gladly give up his post in the name of honor and duty.

Llewellyn was more visibly shaken by the news. The takeover battle had been the crowning glory of his career, and if he had shot himself in the foot more than once, well, at least he did so in a blaze of glory. Saving Sotheby's on the way to saving his own skin had been his mission, and at least he thought he had done the job well.

With Thompson, Westmorland, and Wilson leading the campaign, Sotheby's would appear to be a different firm: cooler, calmer, less worked-up, and caring only for the public interest, not their own skins. Their efforts would be directed to members of Parliament, especially to the more powerful senior members. The goal would be to get the ear of Lord Cockfield, for the trade minister had the power to override the decision of Borrie in the Office of Fair Trading; and as of April 24, it looked as if Borrie would allow the Sotheby's bid to pass without further delay. First thing Monday morning, the new faces at Sotheby's would present the argument to him and others close to Cockfield.

The youthful dynamism of GJW fired the crew with new

energy. There was in fact no time. The pace would be break-
neck. While Thompson and Westmorland met with government
officials Monday morning in Whitehall, over in Warburg's an-
tiseptic green fluorescent-lit offices, Stevenson and his team put
the finishing touches on the official Sotheby's response to the
GFI/Knoll bid. Wilson did some meeting of his own, since he,
better than anyone at Sotheby's, knew how government chains
could be pulled.

The performances were brilliant. Meeting with Minister of
Arts Paul Channon in his Whitehall office, Westmorland put
on one of the shows of his life. Thompson hobbled in on a cane,
only adding to the dramatic appeal, and sat graciously through
the meeting while Westmorland used him as a foil. "Here is one
of the world-ranking scholars in the field of Chinese art," the
Master of the Horse said effusively. When he spoke to those
outside the peerage, Westmorland often exercised the deferential charm adopted by some aristocrats to bring us closer to them
while at the same time sustaining the barrier of rank. "I don't
see how," he said, "we can afford to lose someone as valuable
as Julian. He knows more about Chinese art than almost anyone in the world, and he has said he will be forced to resign in
the event of this take-over. This is not in the public interest—
do you think? It is not in the interest of the arts in Great Britain."

The arts minister was duly impressed, but there was little
he could do except talk to others about the Sotheby's case. As
in America with the National Endowment for the Arts, those in
charge of such programs hold relatively little power. Fortunately the firm found other allies. Patrick Cormack, Conservative MP and chairman of the All Party Heritage Committee, who
lists his recreation in *Who's Who* as "fighting philistines," rallied a group of MPs behind Sotheby's on Monday. Claiming that
Sotheby's was a national treasure—like Westminster Abbey or
the Tower of London—which should be preserved at all costs,
Cormack raced around the House of Commons, buttonholing a
small but influential cross-party group interested in trade and
arts.

Cormack met with little opposition to his campaign. A rue-

ful Anthony Beaumont-Dark, a Tory who had made his name
by guarding Thatcher's free-trade competition policy, was one
of the few who voiced objections to the idea that the government should involve itself with Sotheby's. "How can Sotheby's
claim to be part of the national heritage," he asked wrily, "when
they have made so much money selling off bits of it?" A very
good point, particularly in light of the gala sale, scheduled for
New Bond Street the following week, of the armor from Hever
Castle which included a vast array of national treasures from
the Astor Collection.

Beaumont-Dark's point was lost on at least six other members of Parliament who would soon call for a vote on the matter. On Tuesday, the following day, Cormack placed a question
in the daily Notices of Questions and Motions, appealing to the
ministers for action. The question: "To ask the Minister of Trade
whether he will take immediate steps to refer the proposed take-
over of Sotheby's to the Monopolies and Mergers Commission."
The question would be placed in Cockfield's box, and he could
or could not, as he saw fit, answer Cormack directly.

The same day, Sotheby's released its defense of the bid.
Coupled with the Cormack question, the defense document cast
some doubt on the likelihood of a GFI victory. The market,
however, had another story to tell. More than a million shares
passed into the hands of the two Americans the same day, and
Cogan and Swid, speaking from their Park Lane headquarters,
said Sotheby's would be theirs before the upcoming Havemeyer
sale in mid-May. Bottles of wine were uncorked in the headquarters of the mavericks, high above Hyde Park greenery and
Buckingham Palace.

*Whatever had become of these British institutions that
would not sell out to Americans?* Brunton must have wondered
to himself as he read the morning's stock quotations. He need
have looked no further than his own defense document, in fact,
for a clue to what had become of them. For there in the twelve-
page professionally printed publication, beyond the plea on the
cover—which read "This letter contains your Directors' unan-
imous advice:— NOT TO ACCEPT the offer from Knoll International Holdings, Inc."—was the reason that hardly anyone had

heeded the advice. Set out in starkly honest terms not even necessary in such a document, the directors concluded: "Upon rejection of the offer, and assuming no new factors emerged, there is a likelihood of a decline in the market value of your shares." They did not speculate how much the value would decline, but anyone in the City could have told them that Sotheby's shares would plummet from the present offer of approximately \$7 per share to roughly half as much without an official bid.

How would you vote?

FOURTEEN

S OTHEBY'S had something else up its sleeve. In warning
shareholders about a decline in the market value of stocks,
the directors also introduced the notion of a "new factor"—a
euphemism for White Knight. No new factors had emerged, as
everyone in the City noted with interest that week, but a new
factor-in-the-making had been doing some touring of the York
Avenue facility around the same time. This White Knight even
had a suntan. Fresh and bronzed from recent winter weekends
in Palm Beach and the Bahamas, he sauntered into the ultramodern auction extravaganza for a meeting with Marion. After
a whirlwind tour of the building and grounds, the two men settled down in Marion's second-floor office for a chat.

This White Knight presented sharp contrasts to Cogan and
Swid. Not the least of which was that there was only one of him,
at least in the beginning. He was big, like a football player over
fifty, packed into a three-piece American-cut suit. The buttons
on his vest reached out as he sat down on the other side of
Marion's antique desk. The two men eyed each other across one
of the auctioneer's prized possessions, an ashtray "embel-
lished," in Sotheby's catalog parlance, with a cluster of white

golf balls. The White Knight wore dark-tinted aviator-style glasses, which added to the impression that he was from Hollywood. He was not from Hollywood, although he had made a bundle in California recently and probably picked up some of the state's more pronounced traits while doing business on the coast.

"I understand you're in trouble," he said slowly to Marion, emphasizing the word *trouble*. This was an understatement, a calculated understatement that served to emphasize a need for cooperation with the White Knight should he choose to draw his lance.

Laughter.

"Well, yes, you might say that we are," Marion said, looking down at his ashtray. The White Knight played golf, too, and the two men had noted happily that they both enjoyed the same sport. Swid plays, too, but Marion would not have known that, for he had never agreed to meet Swid in his office or anywhere else.

"Well, I believe I can help you out."

Pause.

"I can put my finger in the dyke."

The problem was that the White Knight would do no good at all if the unwanted suitors won the battle before he arrived. So it was a great relief for Sotheby's and their high-priced lobbyists when the British government leaned in their direction. On Thursday, April 28, 1983, in another installment of questions and motions for the House of Commons, the following motion (rather than question) appeared. Sandwiched in between a motion on WAR WIDOWS and one on DIRECTORY INQUIRIES was number 472, entitled FUTURE OF SOTHEBYS. The motion, which was a direct appeal to the trade minister, read: "That this House, believing that the proposals of Messrs Swid and Coggan [*sic*] to take control of Sotheby's could threaten the future of that great auction house and endanger London's preeminent position in the world's art market, calls upon Her Majesty's Government to ensure that the proposed takeover be referred to the Monopolies and Mergers Commission forthewith [*sic*]."

A motion carries more weight than a question, and it carries even more weight when it has additional signatures, as this one did. There may be more than a little irony in the number of MPs willing to go for the finish in the Sotheby's battle versus the number willing to risk their careers for the WAR WIDOWS motion. Whereas only six MPs signed the WAR WIDOWS motion, eight affixed their signatures to the FUTURE OF SOTHEBYS. Collecting eight signatures for any move is no small task, but for this move—a direct challenge to the government's laissez-faire attitude toward business—it was nothing short of miraculous.

The glue that bound this bipartisan group, however, was not economic policy but, rather, xenophobic patriotism. Perhaps Brunton had been right all along in his thinking. The only way to repel these invaders from the west would be with the flag. If only the directors had behaved more coolly in the beginning of the battle, then perhaps the government would have gotten a clearer picture of the problem sooner.

Suspense was mounting.

By the end of the week, the directors awaited the trade minister's response with bated breath. It was well known by then that Borrie had sent a "confidential" letter to Cockfield turning down Sotheby's request for a referral. His reasons were, as stated, that he saw no sign of a threat of monopoly in the proposed merger. Cockfield, however, was more inclined to reject the decision of his director than most ministers were. He had acquired a reputation for shooting from the hip. As one of Thatcher's inner circle of ministers, moreover, he was likely to take the matter up with the Prime Minister. The upcoming June election, which would be waged under the banner of renewed patriotism and growth of British industry, would doubtless weigh on their decision. Or would it?

In interviews from their Park Lane headquarters, Cogan and Swid attacked the defense document, pointed out errors of fact in it, and concluded that the opposition was "in some disarray." In response to the Thursday motion, GFI/Knoll took out a full-page ad in several daily newspapers. The unwanted suitors would, the ad declared in boldface type, "respect the name of the firm, and the essential Englishness" of it. They would restore profitability and they would work with those experts who wanted to work with them. Both shareholders and staff members had moved to their side, and with or without the directors' help, the two Americans felt certain they would assume control of the firm.

The marauders laid out a plan for a smooth transition in the likely event of early victory. Their shadow board would slip into place smoothly with several key figures at its head. Aside from Lord Harlech, who had already been named in early talks about the take-over, there was a probability that two of Sotheby's current directors would join the two Americans: Peter Wilson and Angus Ogilvy, the husband of Princess Alexandra. Ogilvy was also named as a possible turncoat, since his name was not on the official petition sent by the staff to the unwelcome suitors. Other members of the British establishment were also rumored to be in talks with them about roles they might assume in the new firm.

More than half the staff, including many of the 133 who had signed the petition, met secretly with the felt merchants and promised to set aside their earlier threat. The uniformed porters and doormen, who had cried when Wilson retired, were only too happy to see the new owners step in, and they openly rebelled against the management during the last week of the battle, refusing to do their jobs and, in one case, actually dropping something of considerable value.

Normal work all but stopped on New Bond Street and on York Avenue. The flow of consignments had slowed to a trickle, and one of the senior experts in New York complained that he had almost given up: "Why bother making phone calls or visiting clients," he asked rhetorically, "when all they want to talk about is whether Sotheby's will be here tomorrow? This is depressing and I want it to end now." Unlike a manufacturer, which could continue to churn out widgets even during a take-over battle, Sotheby's made no product. Its produce was a service, provided to buyers and sellers on the basis of trust. The battle had clearly taken its toll; and the trust had all but vanished in the wind of talk in the government, the City, at smart parties in Belgravia, over the FUTURE OF SOTHEBYS.

One of the Jewish staff experts in New York complained

that she spent most of her time assuaging the fears of her Jewish clients. "No, this does not mean that we are anti-Semitic
here," she says she repeated over and over. "It's just that the
board, it seems, doesn't like these particular people. It wouldn't
matter to them if they were Moslem or Seventh Day Adventist.
I know it sounds like a case of racial prejudice. No, that's not
what they meant by 'the wrong kind of people.' No, I haven't
met them, but really, do you know anyone who has?"

Through their banker Seelig, the two Americans told the
press that a referral, should Cockfield decide on one, would only
further damage Sotheby's business prospects. Cogan dismissed
the talk that Sotheby's had begun discussions with an unidentified White Knight. He dismissed it because such talk is a common tactic during unwanted-take-over battles. The goal is to
undermine the confidence of the suitors and sway shareholders
to hold on to their vote, with the prospect of a higher bid.
Sotheby's, as far as he could tell, had been in constant talks
with all sorts of White Knights from the beginning of the GFI
attack, even before. There was no reason for him to believe that
this White Knight was any more than a phantom.

On Wednesday, May 4, Cogan was humming in his suite at
the Park Lane, awaiting an early breakfast date, when the phone
rang. It was Seelig calling from Morgan Grenfell. The two men
had become friends during the battle and they found their daily
phone conversations a source of pleasure. This morning Seelig
found it difficult to exchange small talk, and his voice was
strained and upset. He found it difficult to say what he had called
to tell the American. This was the very phone call Seelig had
dreaded for longer than he cared to think. He was certain he
had prepared the two Americans for its possibility, but from
the sound of Cogan on the other end, he had not.

"Cockfield just announced he would refer your bid to the
Monopolies and Mergers Commission for further study."

"On what grounds?"

"He doesn't need any. I told you that, I believe."

"Didn't he say anything?"

"He said he was referring the bid to the commission to de-
termine whether this merger was in the public interest, owing

to the great public interest in the bid." Seelig mocked the trade minister's words.

"Public interest?"

"Right."

"Can we appeal?"

"No."

"Shit."

"Sorry."

Cogan was shocked. While he had been warned of the possibility of a referral by the mercurial trade minister, the odds had been clearly against it. Of the thousands of bids that had crossed his desk since he joined the government, Cockfield had overturned only five others. There was something fishy going on, and Cogan was determined to get to the bottom of it. This was not supposed to happen. *Whose word in which ear?* would be a topic of London conversation for months, years.

Cogan then surprised himself with his reaction: He put the phone back in its cradle and nearly started to cry. It's no fun to lose, even under the best of circumstances—which these clearly were not. *The Park Lane has a good wine cellar*, he thought as he phoned room service for a bottle of Pouilly-Fumé 1974, the very wine in which he had toasted victory only the night before.

Though he rarely has more than a few glasses of wine with dinner, the buzz of drinking first thing in the morning, on an empty stomach, made him feel light-headed, relaxed, and fortified. He dialed the phone and booked a seat on the 10:30 Concorde to New York. He had to get out of England. The whole affair had turned into a public humiliation. He tried to stop himself from thinking about the referral, but his mind would not cooperate.

A moroseness gripped him and would not let go. He looked out at the gentle sweep of greenery in Hyde Park, the best of London lying at his feet. He thought about his plans for the following day: Sotheby's was auctioning the contents of Hever Castle. Lord Astor, the man Brunton had gleefully reported would not shake hands with the two Americans, would be there, and Cogan and Swid had planned to be there too. It would have been sweet to greet Astor as the new owner of Sotheby's and watch his face as he reacted to the news. Now it looked as if Brunton and Astor would have the last laugh.

There was no doubt what the referral meant, even though there was much doubt about why it had been requested. Cockfield's decision was binding and there was no appeal. For the next six months a group of experts handpicked from the British business establishment would scrutinize the fitness of the two Americans. The group was an honorary and voluntary one, and they would not rush their decision. They would interview the two Americans and their advisers and co-conspirators. Then they would carefully take a pulse reading, which would lead to a vote. The vote would reflect not only their appraisal of these Americans as fit guardians of the 240-year-old art auction house, but also the fitness of *any* foreign bidder.

During the review period the two Americans would be barred from buying any more stock in Sotheby's, as they already owned the most a single shareholder can legally acquire without a proxy vote—which was of course blocked by the referral. They could keep their 29.9 percent, but they must give up the votes they had received from the shareholders for the remaining shares. Any other foreign bidder would be subject to the same stipulation.

For all intents and purposes the unwanted suitors were back at square one. While Sotheby's had time to build a proper defense, which might involve finding a more suitable White Knight, Cogan and Swid had been stripped of their hard-earned votes and their momentum. Could they start up all over again in six months? What about their financing? Having borrowed to buy the shares at up to 4 percent above prime, each day the takeover was delayed cost them lots of money: "Like a taxi meter out of control—click, click, click," Swid pointed out. But this was not the first time the two seasoned traders had been knocked down, and the consensus then was they would climb back in the ring.

There was little reason to expect the bid to be blocked after the review. Cockfield had bowed to some pretty strenuous pressure, and he was duly reprimanded in the press and in the government. "What is not desirable," the *Financial Times* concluded in an editorial the day after the surprising move, "is for the Secretary of State for Trade to refer bids on the basis of nebulous and arbitrary criteria and to do the Director of Fair Trading out of a job by paying more attention to active lobbying on companies that are down on their luck." The "nebulous and arbitrary criteria" were London's "preeminent position in the international art market and Sotheby's position in relation to that market," as Cockfield had stated in his findings, a position that, the *Financial Times* found, "takes some imaginative effort to build up. . . . The art market has long been thoroughly international; and since Sotheby's under British ownership has taken itself wherever in the globe this business can be found, the xenophobic fears appear misplaced."

The lobbying was another matter. By Sunday the story of the GJW effort would be laid out on the front inside page of *The Times* for all of Great Britain to relish and scorn. Much of the success of the lobbying effort was put on GJW's ability to get to the trade minister, a previously taboo tactic that had not been exploited before. The trade minister denied that he had been actively lobbied. Banker Seelig was incredulous: "I have never in my life heard of such a tactic and would not have advised it for my clients. I don't believe it."

Cockfield was also known to be one of Thatcher's closest confidants. "He thinks in paragraphs," the Prime Minister once said glowingly of her minister. Cockfield may have made other decisions without conferring with his first minister, but there is little doubt he talked over the Sotheby's problem with her, primarily because it had received so much attention. Seelig claims that his sources at Number 10 Downing Street all led him to believe she would not interfere with the bid. "Sotheby's had made its own bed," he said he understood her to think. "Let them lie in it."

But Cockfield would not have gone against Thatcher's advice at this point in his career. Although he had enjoyed her confidence, by now his power was waning, although few would know how impotent he had become until after the June reelection of the Thatcher government. Cockfield would not be reappointed trade minister but would be made a minor minister in the government and would serve out his term in relative obscurity.

Cockfield would not have disobeyed Thatcher's advice, the thinking went, but what if the advice was handed down from an authority higher than the Prime Minister? What if the Queen herself, strange as it may seem to those accustomed to the postage stamp theory of monarchy rule, told Cockfield to refer the Sotheby's bid? In the U.K. the queen's right to make decisions without explanation is considered, naturally, sovereign: above or greater than all others, unchallenged. And there are several good reasons why Sotheby's would have attracted the attention of Elizabeth II.

With Westmoreland a close member of the royal household for more than twenty-five years, the Queen would have had ample opportunity to discuss the Sotheby's matter during the preceding months. Like many of her subjects, she was probably confused as to what was going on over at New Bond Street, with all the talk about blowing out brains and wrong kind of people, and she probably sought to find out, even if she did not instruct Cockfield to refer the bid. As a collector—in fact the Queen is the largest single private collector in the world—she would have other reasons for an active interest in the market for art and London's position in that market. She had probably heard talk that London was losing its preeminence to New York and would want to stem the tide, even though her Prime Minister may have disagreed with her.

The very thought of Her Majesty reading the Sotheby's defense document through the eyeglasses she uses when she opens her government each summer is intriguing. The press office in Buckingham Palace summarily dismissed all thought on the matter, and only one of the many journalists analyzing and covering the saga of Sotheby's even ventured to bring up the theory, presenting it somewhat obliquely, as follows: "GOD SAVE THE QUEEN," wrote columnist Patrick Sergeant in the May 5 issue of the *Evening Standard,* "and all her relations, and keep us in our proper stations. Let this text, hand-embroidered, hang as a warning to those who would lay impious hands on our great national institutions—which, from today, include Sotheby's, the sale-rooms."

Sergeant did not say that the Queen had a hand in the referral. He only seized the opportunity to begin his column with the reference, the point being that Her Majesty's government, notably her minister for trade, possessed spellbinding power and perpetuated an unfair class system. This was normal left-wing rhetoric, of the sort that would be expected from an iconoclast like Sergeant, an ardent defender of people like Cogan and Swid and a widely respected sharp-tongued wit whose mind penetrates often right to the core in fewer than five hundred words. Between the lines, Sergeant was presenting the royal theory, but he could get away with it because he would be expected to present such a theory anyway. He was not alone in his thinking, however. Banker Roger Seelig adhered to the royal theory, too, as the only plausible explanation.

On his return to New York, Cogan drove straight to Southampton on eastern Long Island. Away from family, friends, nosy reporters, and meddlesome queens, he holed up alone in the rambling fourteen-room shingled "cottage" where he spends weekends most of the year. Here among the sprawling Gatsby-esque mansions, in the land of swans and croquet, where houses still have names and servants still use the back door, at least he knew what the rules were.

PART III

THE WHITE KNIGHTS

FIFTEEN

AUCTIONS of medieval artworks ordinarily draw a small crowd of assorted eccentrics. The sale of the contents of Hever Castle was another matter. By 9:00 A.M., when the uniformed guards opened the double doors of the New Bond Street salesroom, a mob of curiosity seekers stood outside awaiting another installment of the decline and fall of the House of Astor, as though it were live soap opera, upscale.

They were not disappointed.

Lord and Lady Astor appeared outside the Regency white facade soon thereafter. The British appetite for stories of "domestic crises" and how the hons do with less than they had before seemingly knows no bounds, as anyone who has watched an evening of British television will attest—and this one had all the right elements. The kindly medieval art specialist with the shock of bushy blond hair greeted the couple and led them to the front of the room. They glanced around approvingly: There was no sign of the unwanted suitors nearly everyone referred to by the code names Bubble and Squeak.

Not that the sale of Hever and dispersal of its contents had gone smoothly so far. As in the sale of Sotheby's, there had been outcries from historic preservationists over the loss of what could truthfully be called "one of England's great treasures." Unlike the take-over laws, however, the laws governing real estate are quite clear. The baron could put his property on the market, Britain being a property ruling nation, but he would have to wait for a British bidder who wanted to preserve the estate and castle. After several years and many hours of discussion, a property developer had finally purchased the castle through Sotheby's realty division for a reported £9 million sterling, or roughly $13.5 million, excluding the rare armor and medieval artifacts for sale today, May 5, 1983.

The Arthurian theme park and mock armory were being dismantled and scattered to the wind, but Astor did not seem to mind, though Lady Astor said with feminine sensitivity that the sale was "agonizing." Only the week before, the tenant farmers and loyal retainers on the three-thousand-acre estate had protested publicly. A seventy-six-year-old widow, recovering in the hospital from a stroke, claimed that she woke up one morning to find her farm sold out from under her, and herself with no place to go. And several others claimed that the property developer, Broadlands, Ltd., had gone back on its word to offer them the first right of refusal for the property they had rented from Lord Astor and farmed. Where was the White Knight, one wonders, for the victims of this sale?

The sale began with a quick rap of the gavel from the elegant auctioneer. Pocketbooks opened as wide as some mouths as the prices began to bounce off the ceiling. Even the prosaic lances and crossbows, which had furnished the mock armory at Hever by the thousands, fetched prices higher than Sotheby's had anticipated, and there was the heady good feeling of big money and the momentum it can create in a salesroom. Boom, boom, boom, down it went. Money, money, money—in pounds, dollars, yen, deutschmarks, Swiss francs.

The big thrill of the two-day marathon arrived shortly after lunch on the first day, in time for the important transatlantic phone hookups Sotheby's had provided for a few important American bidders—it being 9:00 A.M. on the Eastern Seaboard at 2:00 P.M. in London. Several well-tailored young attendants

manned the red phones beside the podium and relayed their
clients' bids to the auctioneer. The air was charged with electricity as the sale of a rare sixteenth-century armor suit got under way. Lady Astor cocked her head upward and held out her
eyeglasses, brushing them pensively against her lower lip. Lord
Astor stood like an old soldier, upright and stony-faced, seemingly nonplussed by a woman behind him who was gaping without self-restraint.

Bidding began at £100,000 sterling, or roughly $150,000.
This suit was no ordinary suit, and Sotheby's anticipated it would
fetch as much as £500,000 sterling, or roughly $750,000, more
than any other had before. A one-of-a-kind display suit, made
for beauty instead of battle, the richly ornamented and gilded
costume originated in the collection of Henry II of France; it
was handcrafted in the 1540s by Giovanni Paoli Negroli, a
Milanese craftsman whose work was of consistently high quality. But no one could have known the fierce battle it would
touch off.

Within seconds rather than minutes, the bids had climbed
beyond £500,000. As the auctioneer called out one million pounds
sterling, the rest of the room seemed to join the gaping woman
behind Lord Astor in disbelieving jaw-dropping. The baron remained cool. Up and up the price soared, passing the £1.5 million mark with barely a nod from the auctioneer, and all but
two telephone bidders dropped out of the contest. The attendants spoke in whispers to the telephonic buyers competing with
one another from miles away, through mere copper-wire hookups, against the crackle of the ever-present static on British
telephone equipment.

Bids were placed in £250,000 levels, moving to £1.6 million
without hesitation. Then the action slowed down for the final
push: £1.7 million. The auctioneer repeated the last bid over
and over in a broad English accent, drawing the words slowly
from his throat, lulling the crowd into an avaricious trance. One
of the two attendants nodded slowly: £1.725. Quickly, £1.75.
The only sound in the room was the attendant's furtive whisper
to the underbidder as he attempted to size up his opponent. No
one in the room could believe what was happening. Once, twice,

three times, like a boxer down for the count, the underbidder had only minutes to regain his courage before the round—and the metal suit—was lost to him and won by someone else.

Sold!

Lord Astor managed a wry smile. The family's heirloom had fetched nearly four times what he had been told it would bring. Adding Sotheby's 10 percent buyer's premium, the sixteenth-century suit of armor brought £1.925 million, roughly $2.8 million. The buyer, whose identity Sotheby's protected for the first few weeks, would be paying in dollars. He was initially thought to have been an official in the Reagan administration, Ronald Lauder, an heir to the Estee Lauder cosmetics fortune and deputy assistant secretary of defense. But Lauder was the under-bidder.

Speculation over the identity of Sotheby's own White Knight took up many inches of British newsprint. There was little concrete information to go on; instead, reporters drew wild conclusions based on who they saw coming and going in the salesrooms. The old list of potential buyers of the troubled firm was all but abandoned. Instead, Barry Trupin, an American nouveau riche tax-shelter magnate who would later become the cause célèbre of Southampton over a battle to complete a $35 million castle, surfaced in the London *Times* as a possible candidate the week after he revealed himself as the mystery buyer of the $2.8 million suit of armor.

Trupin and his armor would eventually make a big splash in high circles in Britain, but not because he was the mystery knight riding over the hill to save Sotheby's. Before he could remove his new acquisition from Great Britain he would have to wait for an export license. One of the conditions of the license was that he wait a period of time for a British buyer to surface and match his bid, a formality required by law for treasures of national importance, even though the suit was made in Italy for a French king and brought to England by an American expatriate of German descent. No buyer surfaced, but the sale caught the attention of the heir to the throne, the Prince of Wales, a fellow armor enthusiast who invited Barry and Renée Trupin for dinner.

But Sotheby's was not issuing dinner invitations. The firm was issuing a license to buy into what they still considered "one of the great treasures of the nation." And there was little time for laughing or delaying. Starting with the Astor sale, the art market had quickly begun its climb from a two-year slump. Recessions in the art market, according to Teather & Greenwood, a London stock analyst that follows the auction houses, tend to be brief but deep. Now that the recession was ending, all sorts of sellers who had delayed until the market recovered its strength would be rushing to the auction houses; or, until Sotheby's settled its problems, to Christie's.

No one was more painfully aware of this than Peter Wilson, the architect of the modern auction system and "the price of art will only go up." Wilson's theory, which had proven true to some extent for more than twenty years, allowed for recessionary dips. He called them "hiccups." As negotiations were about to begin for the Florence Gould estate—the $200 million prize that Wilson hoped would be the feather in his cap—he urged the directors to enter into serious talks with anyone, or at least someone. The others might be supercilious, but Wilson was willing to throw in his pride for the sake of business, as was Westmorland, who took most of his advice from his elder cousin.

Cogan and Swid were not going to vanish just because their bid had been put on hold. Having recovered after the devastating news, Sotheby's largest shareholders announced from New York that they would finish pursuing the course they had begun, even though it meant more work and more money. For the sake of appearances, Cogan was petitioning the Securities and Exchange Commission to drop all charges against him. He would have done that originally, he said, but the cost at the time would have been prohibitive. The laws had been softened since the charge was levied, however, and now it would not be as difficult or costly.

Cogan was thinking about all this as he walked through Sotheby's York Avenue salesroom in the middle of May. He was in the starkly modern auction house to see the Havemeyer Collection of paintings. Havemeyer, the sale that begins this book, would be quite a remarkable one, as you may recall; and Cogan wanted a chance to see what it was all about and to reaffirm his position during the presale viewing period when thousands would swarm through the place on their way to brunch or Bloomingdale's. "Hi, how are you doing?" he greeted friends and fellow art buffs. "Yes, we are still intending to go ahead with our bid." He probably had no idea that the head of the paintings department would later describe his performance there in scathingly snobbish terms: "like a grubby little shopkeeper, rubbing his hands as though he owned the place."

Given all that has gone on in the poor besieged operation, the Havemeyer sale was more than a resounding success; it was a miracle. Whatever the reasons for it, the Havemeyer sale would long be remembered as the record $38 million turning point in Sotheby's fortunes, even though no one really knew it beforehand.

Hoarse with strain and red-faced and puffy from the lights, Marion seized the opportunity to address the press with good news for a change. With grace and humor he answered the questions posed by reporters who had been assigned to cover an auction without knowing who Degas was. There were lots of questions, though curiously none of them were about the takeover battle or search for a White Knight. Marion sipped at a glass of scotch, puffed on a long brown cigarette, Clint Eastwood-style, and surveyed the room for those he knew to be unsympathetic to Sotheby's plight.

"I just want you to know," he said admonishingly, "that this proves we can do something right."

Pause.

"Who said you couldn't . . . ?" Sourien Melikian of the *International Herald Tribune* asked coyly.

". . . hold an auction," finished Isolde McNicholl, then editor of *Art and Auction*.

SIXTEEN

L ONDON is a major stop on the American millionaires' summer circuit. Each June, at the races in Ascot, the flower show in Chelsea, the antiques show at the Grosvenor House Hotel, rowing at Henley, Americans spread their hard-earned dollars and perpetuate the golden myth of the land of opportunity and Horatio Alger.

So it was no surprise to anyone when Mr. and Mrs. A. Alfred Taubman booked into a second-floor Art Deco-style two-bedroom suite in Claridge's Hotel on Brook Street off New Bond near Sotheby's main salesroom. Few people had heard of Alfred, the Detroit property and fast-food magnate who had just completed the largest deal since "the Louisiana Purchase," as he liked to tell people who hadn't heard of him. His syndicate of investors turned over $1 billion on a $300 million investment in the Irvine Ranch in the Southern California megalopolis in only a matter of years. Others called the deal "the toughest battle in the West since Little Big Horn," and Taubman was known back home in Michigan as a rough operator. London in June is full of similar stories out of the States, not to mention Saudi Arabia and Kuwait.

Judy Taubman was better known in London as Judy Mazur, her maiden name, or Judy Rounick, her first married name, under which she had worked at Christie's in Geneva, in London, and in New York, where she met her second husband, Alfred. A striking blonde with high cheekbones, she has a cosmopolitan manner (she is fluent in seven languages, including Hebrew) that won her a crown as Miss Israel in the early sixties (although the Israelis claim there are no records of the winners). Her recent marriage to Taubman was no surprise to anyone, because she had always claimed her second husband would be richer than her first, a Seventh Avenue man of no small means. "I knew Judy twenty years ago in St. Tropez," a fellow traveler said in Chelsea, "and I thought then, 'There's a *very* aggressive girl from Tel Aviv,' and I am not going to be surprised by anything she does."

On this trip, Judy rode out to Canterbury in a hired Bentley to attend an auction. Christie's was selling the contents of Godmersham Park in a "house sale" in a tent on the grounds of the rolling green estate. An eighteenth-century brick Georgian mansion furnished luxuriously with rare needlework and eighteenth-century French furniture of the quality normally found in museums or embassies, Godmersham Park was reputed to be the setting for Jane Austen's novel *Mansfield Park*. Judy plunged into a bidding battle for a pair of rare needlework pillows against another American millionairess. By the end of the heated contest, Mrs. J. Seward Johnson, better known as "Basha," widow of the son of the founder of Johnson & Johnson, was forced to pay $21,000. It was a record price for a pair of pillows. Still no one raised an eyebrow.

Judy was not the only attendant and spotter from Christie's to marry well, or at least into money. Her friends wished her good luck; they remembered her kindness and they remembered how lost she had seemed in the workaday world. Now, she could come to London and bid at auction for pillows. At least that was why everyone thought she had come to town. Even the salesroom correspondent for *The Times* of London, hot on the trail of the mysterious White Knight, failed to make any connection as she interviewed Mrs. Taubman in Godmersham Park.

But while Judy was motoring around London in the black shiny Bentley, husband Alfred was deep in talks with Sotheby's and about to lift his visor as the White Knight who would join in battle with the unacceptable suitors. He did so on the morning of June 10, the day after Margaret Thatcher won her second term as Prime Minister.

"You have no idea what this means for a person like me," Taubman said respectfully. "Why, it's like coming over here and buying the crown." He was a big man, given to big pronouncements, but there was something bigger than life about this American. There was something revealing about his hands. A clue lay in the black-and-white pictures he handed out for official purposes: Beneath the smile on the tanned oval face—a full face fringed by wiry gray hair, American executive-style—both hands were tightly wound into a well-sprung fist.

The White Knight was a boxer. Not a professional, but an amateur who works out with a trainer for forty-five minutes each morning before breakfast, in his basement in suburban Bloomfield Hills, Michigan. Taubman, a modern man who knows trends, calls the workout "good aerobic exercise," but those who met him the first week in London, or before, know there is more to it than that. Since a gentleman never makes a fist unless he intends to knock another's block off, the fist in the portrait takes on added significance.

A. Alfred Taubman began life sixty years ago in Pontiac, Michigan. The youngest of four children of German-Jewish immigrant parents, young A. Alfred was handicapped in more ways than one. He was a poor student, due to undiagnosed dyslexia that made reading and writing, the basic classroom skills, nearly impossible. He turned this liability into an asset by developing his visual creative side, spending most of his time drawing and designing another world where there would be room for a stutterer who was neither an athlete nor a brain. As an undergraduate at the University of Michigan, he juggled time-intensive architecture studies with part-time jobs, "doing things like sell-

ing shoes and working in the construction business." Few remember the tall and bowlegged architecture student from
Pontiac; few, that is, except his college sweetheart, Reva, whom
he dropped out of school to marry in the late forties.

In 1950 he formed the Taubman Company with a $5,000
bank loan from the Manufacturers National Bank of Detroit.
Knee-deep in mud and the rough-and-tumble of postwar Detroit, the Taubman Company started at the bottom of the construction ladder, developing parking lots in the suburbs. Of all
northern industrial cities, Detroit was probably hardest hit by
the urban decay and racism of the fifties; new, shiny, white
suburbs spilled out from the western boundaries as whites fled
to settle in tracts of houses serviced by shopping centers. Taubman, the parking lot developer, made the natural transition to
shopping centers, although he did not do it alone. "I am a self-
made man," he says proudly, "although my parents had a hand
in it." His father, particularly, had "a hand in it," for he was
pressed into service as the field supervisor while Taubman did
the negotiating back in the headquarters in Troy, Michigan.

By 1960, Taubman was a millionaire but an outsider in a
town still rigidly restricted along class and religious lines. A New
York museum curator who worked frequently in the Detroit In-
stitute of Art during this period remembers him unkindly as "a
well-fed restaurateur, I believe, who didn't know how to use a
fork. He wanted 'in' on the art game in the worst sort of way."
It wasn't until 1974 that Taubman struck a gold vein that would
elevate him to national prominence and finally, by 1983, with
his bid for Sotheby's, international fame. Both of which would
make museum curators want "in" on the Taubman game in the
worst sort of way.

By the late seventies Taubman was deep in conversation
with Philippe de Montebello, director of the Metropolitan Museum of Art. Smooth, tall, dark, and handsome, Paris-born De
Montebello has the kind of good looks and sycophantic charm
that have made him the matinee idol of the blue-haired ladies
who fancy art. The conversation is taking place in the Taubman apartment in the grandiose Pierre Hotel in midtown Manhattan. Stephen Swid and Marshall Cogan are there at the large

cocktail party, too. Taubman is enjoying himself enormously, as he particularly does at his own parties, and De Montebello is charmed by his host. Suddenly someone taps Taubman on the arm and tells him he should pay attention to one of his other guests. "The guy's a little tight, Al, and he's leaning against your Rothko."

Paintings by Mark Rothko, one of the chief practitioners of the abstract expressionist movement (he committed suicide in 1970), have sold for as much as $2 million privately. Taubman may not have paid that much for his Rothko, but he knows that the picture would be considerably reduced in value if someone should put his elbow through the middle of the canvas of subtly hued pools of color. He also knows that De Montebello is particularly impressed by large sums of money and by signs of generosity, or what another Met official once called "*true* charity." After a moment's thought, he looks at the informant and says in a deep drawl, "Awww, don't worry about it. I've got eight more of them back home [in Michigan]."

The drawl was acquired, say friends, on the ranch, the gold vein that made such truly charitable talk possible. The ranch was not just any ranch. It was an 80,000-acre working ranch in the middle of the Southern California sprawl, thirty miles south of Los Angeles and fifty miles north of San Diego, named for its founder, Scottish-born pioneer James Irvine. It was purchased for pennies an acre in the 1870s, and by the 1960s small houses on less than a quarter acre in nearby Newport Beach were going for as much as $500,000, and some of the Irvine heirs were itching to speed up the dispersal of the ranch. Unfortunately, it was tied to a complicated foundation set up by James's son J.I., on his death in the late forties, "to preserve the ranch and its place in California life."

The itching actually started in 1959 when Myford Irvine, J.I.'s brother and successor, was discovered in the basement of his mansion dead of two shotgun wounds in the stomach and one in the head. The death was officially ruled a suicide. Soon thereafter, J.I.'s daughter and major shareholder in the foundation, Joan Irvine Smith, began a famous battle for control of the ranch that would last for more than twenty years. *Forbes* in its listing of the five hundred richest in America says Smith's money comes from "real estate and law suits." She sniped at the directors of the foundation, close friends of her father's and uncle's, calling for removal of the "old bozos" on grounds of "gross mismanagement." The $800,000 annual dividend she called "peanuts." The, "feisty, four-times-married Mrs. Smith," as she became known in the press during the widely publicized battle, had few allies until she met Taubman in 1974.

A showdown battle had begun—the board privately tried to sell out to Mobil Oil for $200 million. Smith promptly went to court and filed suit against the "old bozos," charging a "sweetheart" deal. While the suit was pending, Taubman organized an investor group to bid on the ranch. Having discerned, sometime before, the merits of other people's money, Taubman made a specialty of organizing investor groups, as Sotheby's would soon discover. Smith joined the group, along with Henry Ford II, after the opening bid was placed for the ranch. The group, which became known as the Ford Group, also included Charles Allen, the New York investment banker who was involved with Columbia Pictures during the forged-check scandal that exposed David Begelman's unsavory side. Max Fisher, the retired chairman of United Brands and a Detroit philanthropist, was another member of the Ford Group, along with several smaller investors.

Arguing that Taubman and Smith were motivated by the sort of greed J. I. Irvine had expressly tried to avoid in his plan to save the ranch through orderly development, the Irvine Company officials attacked the Ford Group as the "last of the Robber Barons." The group's financing, they claimed, could only be repaid through rapid growth, which would undermine the master plan laid out by J.I. With only $75 million in collateral, the Wells Fargo Bank of California agreed to advance at least $300 million to the group. Environmentalists, a particularly powerful force in California at the time, joined the opponents of the Ford Group, arguing that the wildlife areas of the ranch, among the last in Southern California, would be destroyed by the "crooks from back east" who had linked hands with Smith. Smith was also suspected of having abandoned California, since

she spent most of her time in Middleburg, Virginia, where she
rode with the hunt.

The battle lasted for more than two years. Smith, a handsome blonde in her early forties, led the fray, but Taubman
picked up the slack. Smith called the directors "slovenly and
incompetent," and after filing one of her countless suits against
them, turned to reporters and said with a smile, "They ain't
gonna like it." Taubman was harsher: He promised to "sack"
all of the directors when the Ford Group succeeded with its bid,
which he was confident they would.

Taubman was confident because his field was real estate;
Mobil's was processing oil, manufacturing. "Real estate is eval-
uated in assets," he told *The New York Times* in a rare interview afterward, "but corporations that manufacture goods are
handled on the basis of earnings per share. You can't evaluate
an asset company that way. Mobil was trying to buy Irvine as
a company that made $17 million. And that's how they came up
with, in our opinion, a $40-a-share maximum. I assumed that
was going to be about their authority, and we thought it was
worth more."

In 1977 the Ford Group bid $337 million for the 80,000-
acre ranch. The bid was unchallenged. After a five-year Southern California real estate boom, with the prices of some beach-
front houses doubling every two years, the Ford Group sold out
to developer Donald Bren for a cool $1 billion in early 1983.
For some time after the 1977 victory, Taubman kept a facsimile
of the Wells Fargo Bank $337 million check. No such facsimile
of the $1 billion check hangs over his desk, but he wore it around
his neck, in a sense, on June 10 in London. One London reporter was awestruck by the figure and by the type of deal, which
reminded him, he later said, "of that TV show *Dallas*," the most
popular series at the time in Great Britain. "A billion bucks for
a ranch!" he exclaimed, imitating an American accent as the
British hear it, like a daytime TV announcer.

Okay. Taubman is rich. He talks in numbers only those in
goernment usually know. He cuts an impressive figure. But why
does he want Sotheby's? Sotheby's is not an asset-rich company, like a real estate development firm out of Southern Cal-

ifornia. Nor is it a fast-food franchise that can be valued by
"simple formulas like earnings per share." It is a high-profile
service company worth at most $20 million, but valued at $100
million, the lowest price the White Knight will have to pay. Here
is a calculated risk very few people are willing to take: a potential loss of $80 million, or more.

The first explanation that surfaced was that he was buying
Sotheby's to please his new bride. He himself had said, while
standing in front of the place: "I only buy what I love, if I can,"
raising his arms like a victor. Judy, buzzing around London with
fabric swatches under her arm and a decorator in tow, did little to discourage such thinking. This reminded those who had
forgotten that her brother, Boaz Mazor, was also sort of involved in the auction business. Boaz's companion, English art
critic John Richardson, headed Christie's New York operation
in the later seventies. Richardson claims he got Judy her job
there after her divorce.

Taubman may have bought Judy a new apartment in New
York, and a beach-front spread in Southampton a few houses
down from the Swids and a short drive from Cogan's. But, he
would later prove through an aggressive campaign to rebuild
the business, Sotheby's was more than a $100 million idle play-
thing purchased to satisfy his new bride. Talk about his private
affairs bothers him. "Let's get this straight," he had recently
snapped at a reporter who asked him a personal question. "This
is about the Taubman Company, not Al Taubman." As for
buying Sotheby's to please Judy, he dismissed such talk with a
wave of an arm: "Gossip!" he snarled.

The thing about Taubman is he is all business. Sotheby's
was a business venture for him, much as it had been for Cogan
and Swid. In fact, Taubman was very much like Cogan and Swid,
only older, bigger, and depending on which figures you consult,
much richer. He, too, saw that Sotheby's could move into other
areas and expand the empire into neglected service areas: insurance, storage, shipping, appraisals, loans, and other areas
untapped by Sotheby's or Christie's.

David Metcalfe probably guided Taubman's thinking in the
insurance area. It had been Metcalfe, after all, who had intro-

duced Taubman to Westmorland in the Bahamas only a few
weeks before. Taubman and Metcalfe had been involved in several intricate insurance deals involving Taubman's shopping
centers. The possibilities for art insurance have been virtually
unexplored, involving personal property that few homeowners'
policies adequately cover and fewer commercial policies fully
cover. Millions of dollars are lost each year due to art thefts
and damage to artworks in shipping and handling. Not to mention that artworks covered by insurance are generally under-
valued, because some of them appreciate at a rapid clip unheard
of in most other areas.

The possibilities are enough to make anyone with an ac-
tuarial mind rub his hands with greed. Sotheby's could monopolize the field of art insurance, taking on the appraising and
insuring of artworks in every museum in the world, in every
collection in the world, in every country in the world, since the
firm already had offices in fifty-six cities on six of seven continents. Sotheby's could—and it still may—monopolize the entire
field of art sales, or at least the auctioning end of the business.
"One thing you must keep in mind," Wilson claims he told
Taubman, as well as Cogan and Swid: "Soon there will only be
room for one auction house and I intend for Sotheby's to
be it."

Wilson took over where Metcalfe left off in the talks. Having tried unsuccessfully to push Cogan and Swid through the
board, he was determined not to let Taubman slip by. Wilson
and Taubman had at least one thing in common: Both were om-
nivorous collectors and insatiable art buyers. Although it is difficult to imagine Taubman saying "Oh, I adore that," as Wilson
often would, there is a look in his eyes when he sees something
he loves that says the same sort of thing. The advantages of an
art collector's buying into Sotheby's should be obvious to anyone with the slightest idea of how the operation works. It would
be like a candy lover buying into a candy shop. Or an opium
smoker buying himself a field of poppies. For buying art is like
a drug for those with the habit, which knows no cure except the
next fix.

Taubman soon came to appreciate all Sotheby's little wrinkles and quirks as potentials for added income and pleasure. His financial advisers—some of them, at least—advised him against making a bid for the firm. And to most financial minds, the firm was more than a calculated risk. It was an outright gamble, as literal-minded Brunton had discovered when he took the reins from Lord Westmorland. But Taubman was the gambler most likely to succeed at the Sotheby's table. He was big and bold and brash and brave. He was more than a White Knight. He was a White Hope.

The main problem with Taubman was that Brunton and the bankers from Warburg's had never heard of him either. And they were not so sure he was different from the wholly unacceptable Cogan and Swid. Once they learned whom Taubman would be working with on the bid, however, they quickly changed their minds. For the name of Henry Ford II means more in the United Kingdom than it does in the United States. Whereas in America, Ford has lagged behind General Motors and competed with Chrysler in a three-way race for the market share of the auto industry, in the U.K., Ford has been the only show in town since the Second World War. "It was sort of like 'Well, who are you?' " Wilson recounted afterward at Château de Clavary, imitating Brunton, for whom he had lost all affection. " 'Well, you don't say! Henry Ford? No, of course you're not Henry Ford. But puuullleeease, doooo come in.' " Brunton refused to discuss the conversations, although he did say that he had balked at Taubman because at first he thought he was an "individual" and not a "company."

The Ford connection is what prompted speculation about the Queen's hand in the referral. As one of the largest employers in the empire, what's left of it, the Fords have a relationship with the Windsors that goes back nearly forty years, spanning several governments, Tory and Labour. Surely Ford could get an audience with the Queen. Or so the thinking went in the City, at least in the offices of Morgan Grenfell; and on Fleet Street, at least in the offices of Patrick Sergeant at the *Evening Standard*. And such thinking could help soothe Cogan and Swid. They could then believe that the situation had been beyond all hope, lobbyists or no lobbyists.

Whether or not Ford had a hand in the referral, only he and the Queen know for sure. Taubman, for one, believes someone from his camp did. "[I] made it clear that [my] interest [in Sotheby's] would only be pursued if [I] were given time to exercise normal due diligence," he later recounted. "The question of Sotheby's was then referred to the Monopolies and Mergers Commission." Clearly, the possibility of a Taubman bid was a factor.

And Ford owed Taubman a favor or two. Having once led the Anglophile jet set during the go-go sixties, by 1975 Ford began to falter. Though he worked tirelessly in Detroit, having rebuilt Ford Motor Company's position from 1943 as few third-generation successors ever have, in his spare time he lived like a randy English aristocrat, and 1975 was the year his past caught up with him: He was arrested for drunk driving in Santa Barbara with soon-to-be third wife Kathleen DuRoss, a Detroit model. "Never explain; never complain," the duly contrite fifty-seven-year-old tycoon told reporters, borrowing a line the Duke of Windsor had used some forty years before about another matter.

By 1978, Ford was complaining and explaining about more serious matters. His second wife, Christina, was divorcing him for an enormous sum of money. The mogul who put his worth at "$70 million, give or take $10 million" claimed that he did not have cash to give her. He was forced to sell off much of his vast holdings in real estate and artworks, including a room of valuable eighteenth-century furniture and *objets d'art* from his seventy-six-room Grosse Pointe house. Cristina, who tried to seize control of the collection, called the room "a little corner of Versailles." In 1980, in a matter of minutes, his collection of Impressionist and post-Impressionist pictures set a new record at Christie's in New York. Vincent van Gogh's "*Jardin Public à Arles*," the same picture the heirs of Jakob Goldschmidt had sold in 1958 at Sotheby's in London for $369,600, fetched $5.2 million.

To make matters worse, Ford shareholders had sued the chairman over alleged misuse of company funds, including a million-dollar bribe to the government of Indonesia and the use

of insider's information on a land deal he had staked with
Taubman. The shareholders' suit, filed in New York by Roy
Cohn, asked for nothing less than the chairman's $900,000-plus
salary for the year and his removal. The same year Ford fired
Lee Iacocca in one of the most publicized corporate moves in
the history of industrial America. Ford, who lost his temper more
than once during this stressful period, called the charges "a
personal vendetta."

Ford soon shifted gears. The new Ford was a partner in
the Taubman empire. The relationship was golden: Taubman
had the money and Ford had the name. It was no mistake that
even though Taubman organized the deal in California, the Irvine Ranch group was dubbed the Ford Group. The two men
began appearing in public together and Ford was a frequent
houseguest *chez* Taubman in Palm Beach in a Bauhaus-style
hideaway another frequent guest named "The Love Boat." And
if some of Ford's other children and friends did not like the
setup—his daughter Charlotte said pointedly then that Henry
had "flunkies" for friends—they could complain, it seemed, to
the bank. Ford was remaking his fortune.

By 1983, when Taubman expressed interest in Sotheby's,
his "good friend" Ford was right behind him. Unfortunately for
the two Detroit moguls, the matter of Sotheby's was not entirely in their control, in spite of the power Ford wields in the
United Kingdom.

Cogan and Swid also could have a hand in deciding who,
if not themselves, would end up with Sotheby's. With nearly a
third of the company in hand, the two Americans held an ace
that they would not give up easily. Under British take-over law,
whoever bought into Sotheby's would have to deal with them.
Even if the new suitor managed to get as much as 70 percent,
or all the remaining shares outside the GFI camp, the two
Americans would still hold the upper hand. For under the law,
no one can force another shareholder out until he gains 80 percent of the stock, an impossible situation without Cogan and
Swid's 30 percent share.

It was very difficult for the directors to explain why Taub-

man was more acceptable than Cogan and Swid. Like Cogan and
Swid, Taubman was "in trade," meaning businesses outside the
major professions, and there was no "synergy" between Taubman and Sotheby's. All three were art collectors on museum
boards and committees in New York and Israel. But the two
Americans were willing to sell out to this compatriot. "We told
them," Cogan recalled gleefully, "that it had to be a Jew." And
Sotheby's could not work without Cogan and Swid's cooperation.

But that did not mean Cogan and Swid were going to let
Taubman walk away without a fight. After all, you do not bill
yourself as a White Knight unless you intend to back it up with
some brandishing of lances.

The day after Taubman lifted his visor, the unwanted suitors met with their advisers in an office in midtown Manhattan.
They sat at a round table and mapped out their strategy. The
Taubman bid was actually good news for them. In the absence
of a more acceptable suitor, a number of things could have
happened, none of them particularly good. While it is true that
their bid would have cleared the Monopolies and Mergers Commission, it is also true that the bid would have been reduced
significantly in value, since the share price would drop to meet
the decreased interest in the firm. Cogan and Swid would be
stuck with shares they had paid up to 520 pence apiece for
(roughly $7) that might be worth as little as half as much. The
opposite had happened. With Taubman's forthcoming bid,
the share price had climbed and closed at 535 pence on the
first day.

"We should make them fight for it. These guys are loaded
and they are working in concert with each other. We should
raise the bid immediately to a much higher price. Why fool
around when we know they want it and they know we know they
want it. I mean they are already topping your bid in the market today. This means the arbs [arbitrageurs] are in, in a big
way, waiting for the kill."

Seelig was speaking bluntly. "Taubman has already said
that he would top our bid of five hundred and twenty pence.

That means he wants us to play ball, or at least expects us to play ball. I'd be surprised if he did not."

Swid and Cogan were slightly confused by the rules of the game, having never before launched a take-over battle in Great Britain and never had one referred to the government any-where. They wanted to make sure they were doing the right thing. "Can we do this? I mean, aren't we blocked from making a move until the referral is cleared?" one of them wanted to know.

"Hell, no. Taubman's bid will be referred to the take-over panel too. You know that. You are only blocked from increas-ing your pile of shares. I say we should bid six hundred and thirty pence [or roughly $9] a share for the remaining shares.

"There's another thing. These guys are working in con-cert. Taubman never works alone. I think Ford, possibly one or two others, are buying shares, too, while only Taubman's pile will be watched by the Take-over people. We cannot *prove* that he is working in concert with Ford et al., but we can prove he has the directors' shares in his pocket. I move that we ap-peal to the Take-over people to count the directors' shares in with Taubman's shares."

On June 13, GFI/Knoll raised its official bid for Sotheby's to 630 pence per share, close to $100 million. This much was announced in the daily papers and across the business wire ser-vices. The appeal to count the directors' shares in with Taub-man's was held in confidence until the Take-over Panel could meet and discuss its merits. It was likely to be denied, because such an appeal had never been granted before.

Taubman's response was predictably fiery. The GFI move would cost him $20 million in the bidding battle that had started only the week before. This was not, however, an art auction. There was more he could do than merely raise his paddle and wait for the next bid: He instructed Agius to block GFI's move however he could, as quickly as he could.

A quick check with the Take-over Panel brought one tech-nicality to light. GFI/Knoll had failed to gain the approval of the panel before it raised its bid, approval they would need be-fore they could make any move, now that the bid was under review. Agius quickly pointed this out to the panel and to the

shareholders through an official press release. Morgan Grenfell, the official advisers to the two Americans, was reprimanded by the panel, although the offense was viewed as an
oversight; their offer would not be blocked by the panel for this
reason alone.

There was another reason Agius felt that the bid should be
blocked. GFI/Knoll, he argued effectively, could not afford to
raise its bid by $20 million. The bid was a false bid, creating a
market for false shares in Sotheby's at artificially pumped-up
prices, he said. The beauty of this maneuver was that Agius
himself was blocking the move with something of a bluff. There
was no way he could have known exactly what the GFI/Knoll
financial position was at this time. Perhaps they had induced a
new investor to join them or arranged for some additional financing.

The false-market claim was accepted for review by the Take-
over Panel, and the new GFI/Knoll bid for Sotheby's was blocked
temporarily until the panel could be convinced that financing
existed to back the bid. Cogan and Swid were summoned to
London to prove that they could pay an additional $20 million
for Sotheby's.

By the end of the week, the Take-over Panel handed down
its ruling on the GFI/Knoll request to count Taubman's shares
together with the directors'. This was important for the two
Americans, because it would limit the number of shares Taubman could buy during the review period by several million. Unfortunately, the Take-over Panel denied the GFI request, but
the two Americans appealed the ruling again, to strengthen their
position.

Even with the false-market claim under review, the market
responded favorably to the impending increase in share price.
Cogan and Swid would be allowed to raise their stake, the
thinking went in the City—and on Wall Street in particular,
where most of the buying was then taking place. By the end of
the week, Taubman had been forced to pay as much as 620 pence
per share for several million shares in the money-losing firm.
Even if Cogan and Swid were to be denied their increase, the
minimum bid Taubman could place under British take-over law

was now 620 pence per share. With a 10 percent stake in the firm (possibily more, considering that Ford and Max Fisher, another member of the Detroit group of multimillionaires, could have been adding shares under their names), Taubman had a big hand in the place already; and he was not happy with the way the two Americans continued to fight him, as Swid learned that weekend in Southampton, New York.

Swid was walking down leafy Main Street, past Saks Fifth Avenue and Elizabeth Arden, on his way to buy a Sunday *New York Times*. He was going to buy the paper in Silver's, a grand Jewish delicatessen and newsstand of a sort found only in places like Southampton or Beverly Hills. Silver's is more than a newsstand or a place to buy smoked fish; it is an unofficial meeting spot for nearly all of Southampton, except for those who are so private they send their gardeners or drivers out for the morning paper. So Swid was not surprised when he ran into someone who knew about the Sotheby's deal. Nor was he surprised that Herbert (Herbie) Allen, Jr., scion of the Allen & Company New York investment bank (and nephew of Charles Allen) with serious Hollywood connections, had some advice for him on how to handle the deal.

"Hey, Steve."

"Oh, hi, Herbie."

The two men shook hands. Neither of them expected to talk about the weather or their golf game. They are not that close. But they were likely to talk business.

As one of Southampton's doyennes once told a reporter: "We're all into money out here. And if someone's onto something good, we want to know about it. That's why we come here. Why, if we went to Greece or somewhere like that, we might lose all our money. We need to be here, near the source."

Says Allen: "Listen, I hear you are doing a deal with Al Taubman."

"Yeah, me and Marshall are. Sotheby's. In London."

"I hear you are giving him a hard time."

"Awwww, what makes you say that? We're just doing what we have to do. You know, playing the game like we wanna win."

"Al told me you were."

"He did?"

"I have some advice for you: Look out. The guy's a tough number."

"Yeah, okay. Thanks for the advice."

The doyenne continued: "Now take Al Taubman," she said. "We all like him out here. He's into money but he shares his deals with us. We like that kind of money talk."

There are those who claim that Taubman brought more than twenty individual investors into the Sotheby's deal, many of whom were buying up shares before he even made his official bid, only to be joined together in one big package under the name Sotheby's Holding Company. Which may explain why Allen, whose family had invested in Taubman's businesses, would make an effort to buttonhole Swid in Silver's one sunny Sunday in Southampton.

Which may also explain why the Take-over Panel finally sided with the unwanted suitors. In an unprecedented move on the part of the government regulatory board, on Friday, June 26, 1983, the panel ruled that Taubman would have to count his shares with the directors' shares. It was the first time such a ruling had been made, and it wasn't easy getting the government to review the case three times, particularly when the case involved spending the tax money of British subjects on a ruling involving three Americans' buying out one of Britain's treasured institutions. This ruling cost Taubman several million dollars, but it wouldn't have passed unless the panel had suspected he wasn't reporting all of his shares as required by law.

On Wednesday, Cogan and Swid convinced the panel that they had the financing to back the 630 pence bid, costing Taubman a few more million dollars. They did so by offering a public flotation of stock in Knoll under the name Knoll International Holdings Incorporated, or KIHI. So in a way they were bluffing when they originally placed the bid, for it would appear they did not have cash in hand, as the law requires. The Take-over Panel was satisfied, nonetheless. The two Americans maintained that the flotation would raise an additional $58 million for their bid, more than enough to cover the $20 million rise. The share price climbed above 630 pence the next day, in anticipation of a higher bid from the Taubman camp.

Soon Cogan and Swid would have to meet with the review committee and present their side of the story of Sotheby's. The review committee would judge the two Americans' fitness to run Sotheby's, but most of all they would judge whether any American should be allowed to run the firm.

As Cogan and Swid prepared for their first meeting with the review committee, Taubman was discussing strategy with Agius and other advisers. London had turned unseasonably warm, with temperatures passing ninety in a town that lives without air conditioning or ice cubes, neither usually needed except on these rare occasions. Even summer-weight suits, normal business wear in New York and Washington, are rarities here; and the crowded streets around the City begin to take on the odor of sheep droppings, the result of too many perspiration-soaked heavy wool suits jammed too closely together. The Taubman suite in the Claridge's, on the second floor off the main wrought-iron-decorated Edwardian lobby, was not air-conditioned either.

Taubman must have been hot, irritated and frustrated by the deliberations he was enduring in the pursuit of Sotheby's. The two Americans were putting up quite a battle for the place; he hadn't banked on this, although he had to admit he would have done the same thing had he been in their shoes. The thing was that he wouldn't have been. He was a winner. He knew he was a winner. And when he walked into the review committee to meet the members, they knew he was a winner, too. One of them later recalled that he had never seen anything like the performance Taubman put on. There it was, hot, sticky, and uncomfortable. Taubman walked in in a summer-weight suit looking refreshed and collected. He glanced around the room and smiled. Then he greeted each member individually, shaking their hands firmly and saying in a deep drawl, "Hi. I'm Al Taubman. Nice to meet you."

But Taubman knew he could not keep this up forever. So he summoned Cogan and Swid to the Taubman Company's New

York office for a meeting on Sunday, June 26. Taubman did not want the Sotheby's deal to cost him any more money; no more $20 million shocks. Although he knew that Cogan and Swid had a new war chest of $58 million, he also knew they were paying top dollar (or pound) for Sotheby's now. At the present price, Sotheby's would have to clear $10 million a year; it had lost $4 million the year before and showed little sign of doing $14 million this year.

The Sotheby's bid had cost Taubman more than money. Not that he loses sleep over such deals. But one day soon he would wake up in the morning in Bloomfield Hills and realize the sober truth: "I am no longer a private person," he would lament. He was no longer a private person from the moment he lifted his visor as the White Knight who would save Sotheby's. Reporters were calling him day and night in pursuit of the Al Taubman interview. Their readers wanted to know more about this boxer who had made a billion-dollar ranch deal on the coast and counted Henry Ford among his closest friends.

The meeting that would bring Taubman closer to the public eye was called for early afternoon in the midtown Manhattan office of the Taubman Company. Cogan was surprised by the small office, around the corner from the Pierre, where Taubman collected messages and kept a secretary, most of his real work being conducted in Michigan at the world headquarters on Big Bear Road. Until he bought into Sotheby's, Taubman had realatively little work that required him to be in New York. The New York setup was a convenience that enabled him to mix business with pleasure when he was in town for museum board meetings or to attend the big auctions at Sotheby's and Christie's each fall and spring. In order to maintain Michigan state residence, which kept his personal and corporate income tax low, Taubman would have to spend the majority of the year in Michigan.

The smallness of the room bothered Cogan, who works in a room the size of a bowling alley because he suffers from claustrophobia. He also cannot bear facing a wall in a restaurant, and once asked his hostess to move him to a seat facing a hall and doorway, in what she described as "the most peculiar manner." But Cogan could live with his seat facing the wall in a small room this time, because he had the upper hand in the deal about to take place. Taubman knew that he had to work with the two Americans and they knew he knew by the way he began the meeting with some paternal advice.

"I will tell you something."

Cogan cocked his head slightly to the left.

"You should never want anything as badly as you want Sotheby's."

"Stephen and I really believe we have something to offer the company. We both love and respect art and we've both thought for a long time that the art business was something we could develop into even bigger things."

"Yes, but you should never act like that. People can smell it on you. They will make you want to fight for it. I am telling you this from past experience."

Taubman was setting up a dialogue between GFI and himself that would undermine their confidence and smooth the road for his victory. As someone fifteen years older and considerably richer, he was in a position to deliver lectures to his younger and greener compatriots. Never mind that they held the upper hand, by the end of the talks they would be grateful for whatever Taubman gave them.

"You cannot afford Sotheby's. If you think you can play ball against my kind of money, go ahead and try."

"We can try."

"You cannot. I am going to make you a very big offer for your shares and this will be the last offer I will give you. But I will do it on one condition: The next time you should not want anything as badly as you want Sotheby's."

"I think Stephen and I need some time to think this over. We have invested a lot of time and money in this deal and we cannot let it go easily."

"Well, I don't see why you need more time. Surely you've already thought this over and made up your mind."

"We need time. We'll let you know first thing tomorrow morning."

In fact, Cogan and Swid could not continue with the bid. Even with the additional money from the flotation of Knoll, they were losing their shirts. Taubman knew they were bluffing and that he would eventually walk away with the place. This much they knew as soon as he lifted his visor. For reasons that would become only partially clear, Taubman felt that Sotheby's was worth more than anyone would be willing to pay for it, as he had felt with the Irvine Ranch deal. Perhaps he would be wrong this time, but he didn't get to the place where he was worth five million bucks a week without taking risks in the marketplace.

"I don't think we can go on with this."

Cogan and Swid were discussing their next move in private. Should they accept Taubman's bid, they would walk away with about $10 million in cash for their hard work, but if they stuck it out, they might get even more money in the end. As Swid pointed out to Cogan:

"I don't see why we shouldn't go for the big kill at the end. Wear them down. We've come this far. We've risked almost everything."

"I don't think Taubman would allow himself to lose out in public like this."

"Yeah."

"Let's think of this as just revenge for Brunton and Thompson and Westmorland and, most of all, Llewellyn. I think they deserve a dose of Al Taubman."

On Tuesday, June 28, 1983, A. Alfred Taubman of Bloomfield Hills, Michigan, concluded the London part of his American millionaires' summer circuit in Europe by placing a bid of 700 pence a share for Sotheby Parke Bernet, p.l.c., a publicly traded British company older than America as a nation. His bid was subject to approval from the Monopolies and Mergers Commission. His bid had been accepted by Sotheby's directors and by Sotheby's largest shareholders, GFI/Knoll. It was a strange victory if ever there was one. For nearly $120 million, Taubman would take back to Michigan a company with assets of about $20 million, a temperamental staff of about a thousand worldwide, and a history of mismanagement and messy bookkeeping that made earnings tough to squeeze even in the most profitable years.

It was not the kind of British treasure he could put on his mantelpiece and wait for the market to move in his direction, as he could with the *objets* his wife, Judy, had picked up at auctions there that summer. He could not dispose of it when he grew tired of it, not without taking a bath, as they say. Or could he? What would Taubman do with Sotheby's? That was the question most often asked in London and New York and the smart watering holes, where the name is pronounced correctly as SUH-thu-bees; not SOUTH-bees, as the rubes prefer. Why had he paid so much money for the money-loser that no one except a pair of "unacceptable felt merchants" seemed to want?

"They said I paid too much for the Irvine Ranch," the boxer turned knight would say without missing a beat, "and look what happened there." Everyone had to admit that he had a point, and in Southampton that summer, where he rented Princess Lee Radziwill's house for a reported record $30,000 a week, Taubman would become everyone's "favorite money man of the season."

Taubman probably had no idea what he was going to do with Sotheby's. There were, to be sure, certain things he had to take care of. He would move the operation to America and headquarter it in New York, primarily for administrative and tax reasons. He may have felt "like I am buying the crown," but it made more sense for the crown to be in the land of opportunity. He also intended to move Sotheby's back into private hands, away from the eyes of meddlesome shareholders. His business associates Fisher and Ford, having had to deal with litigious shareholders in the Ford Motor Company and United Brands, agreed that there were many advantages in this age to private ownership. In 1978 the three men were named in a suit filed by Ford shareholders which charged them of insider dealing in land in downtown Detroit. Fisher called the claim "nonsense, because I don't even own any land there." Taubman called the charges "wholly without validity or foundation." To buttress his defense, he attacked the complaint's "obvious lack of research and care which resulted in the inaccurate and erroneous identification of myself as 'Morris Taubman.' "

There was also the day-to-day administration of Sotheby's, which Taubman would at least familiarize himself with through the summer. Then there was the California land deal Sotheby's had started under Brunton's cutback scheme. The Los Angeles salesroom had been on the market for a little more than a year. Its sale had been one of the things Cogan and Swid objected to in their original attack on the firm's management. They called the move "shortsighted," and pointed out accurately that L.A. was a growth area and the salesroom had in fact been profitable. By August the salesroom had found a buyer, but before the sale could close, the board of Sotheby's would need the approval of its largest shareholder, GFI/Knoll. The Monopolies and Mergers Commission having not yet approved a take-over by an American, the players were frozen where they had been in June. Taubman placed a phone call to Swid to get his approval.

"Hello. Steve?"

Swid recognized the harsh northern industrial accent immediately. He felt sure it would give way to a western drawl in a matter of minutes, and he was right.

"Oh, hi, Al. How are you?"

"I'm fine, buddy. Fine. How are you?" The voice softened and the drawl began to creep into the pronunciation of the vowels.

"Great. Just great. What can I do for you?"

"Remember that place out in L.A.?"

"You mean the L.A. salesroom?"

"Yeah."

"I remember it."

"Well, we finally got a good offer for it."

"How much?"

"Oh, a little under six [million]."

"Oh, really?"

The Los Angeles salesroom had originally been listed for more than $10 million. At that price, it seemed even to Cogan and Swid that maybe Sotheby's was getting out of the market at the right time. As it turned out, Sotheby's had gotten into the market at the wrong time, just as it began to collapse.

"How much under [six]?"

"Five point two [million]."

"Oh."

"Listen, Steve, I want your man Ronnie to vote your share on this for you. We need your vote before we can close the deal. It's just a formality. I'm sure you'll agree to help me out."

By Ronnie, Taubman was referring to Roger Seelig, the Morgan Grenfell banker GFI had used to negotiate the Sotheby's bid. Seelig would have to vote for Cogan and Swid in absentia, since neither of them was in London at the time and Sotheby's was a London-based publicly owned company—until Taubman got the green light from the Monopolies and Mergers Commission.

"I tell you what I would like you to do, Al."

"What?"

Swid was being playful, now that he had nothing to lose and everything to gain.

"I would like for Graham Llewellyn to call me and ask for my vote on the Los Angeles sale. Could you do that for me?"

"Awww, Steve! You shouldn't conduct yourself that way. You're a young man. You have a lot to learn about the world. You just don't do this to people."

"This is my condition."

"Why? Why do you want to talk to Graham Llewellyn?"

"It's very simple, Al. Revenge."

"You just cannot do this. You don't go around getting revenge from everyone that crosses you. This is petty."

"This is a special case, Al. You know that."

"I can't do business with you if this is how you are going to behave. This is it. I cannot do business with you."

"This is how I am going to behave, Al."

Click.

Two weeks later, Cogan was calling Swid.

"Hey, Steve. This is important. Listen to this: Graham

Llewellyn just called. I told him to call back. I wanted to get you on the line so you could hear him beg."

"Marshall, you know I can't deal with this right now. I have a presentation to make. You dragged me out of a meeting to tell me this? I thought someone had died. You know how important this meeting is."

Swid was in Minneapolis, Cogan in New York. Swid was in Minneapolis to present the virtues of Knoll International to prospective shareholders and stockbrokers. As the two Americans told the Take-over Panel they would do, they offered shares in Knoll in a public flotation out of New York. Swid was on a whirlwind coast-to-coast trip to address the financial communities in key cities. Cogan had been trying all afternoon to get him out of a meeting to tell him about the Llewellyn phone call that Taubman arranged for them. They both wanted to know how Llewellyn's brains were and whether he had blown them out yet.

"But I thought you really wanted to hear him plead for us to vote our share. It was your idea. I couldn't exactly let him begin his act without letting you in on it, could I?"

"No, you're right. Okay. But this could not have come at a worse time. You're going to have to do it yourself. Let me know how he sounds."

The White Knight returned home with his prize the evening of September 14. The commission had approved his bid that morning. After meeting with the staff in London, Taubman jetted across the Atlantic to meet the staff in New York, along with Westmorland, Brunton, and Ford, who joined him for a gala preview party that evening on York Avenue. The timing was a coincidence, the invitations having been sent out weeks before, just as the timing had been coincidental for the original referral the day before the Astor sale. Or had it been?

Taubman was greeted cautiously by the staff in London, many of whom were wondering what made this American more acceptable than the other two. They would remain confused about it for weeks and months to follow. The public Al Taubman was only beginning to form, and the question-and-answer session with the press was an ordeal for him. Jon Nordheimer, London correspondent for *The New York Times*, threw a curve ball midway through the conference. Taubman might have thought he had returned the ball with a hit, but those attuned to body language noticed that it made him uneasy. The question was: "Mr. Taubman, as a collector, what will you do to avoid the appearance of insider trading [at Sotheby's]?"

To which Taubman responded, without much hesitation: "Sotheby's has very strict rules about insider trading. I guess I'll have to bid at arm's length."

That answer would come back to haunt him from time to time over the next two years, but for now he was en route to New York and a much friendlier reception. The New York staff was eager to see their compatriot, and some of them, like Marion, relished the idea of being owned by a fellow countryman who talked bluntly and acted like J.R. Ewing on *Dallas*. Marion made a point of talking to him as though the two had just met at a country club. The talk was not about the price of art or operation at Sotheby's but, as could be expected, football. "I told Al," Marion later recalled gleefully, "that I lost a bet against his Michigan Panthers [football team]. And he told me, 'That just goes to show you should always bet *with* Al Taubman.'"

During the question-and-answer period with the staff—which was closed to the press in the United States, after the debacle earlier in London—Taubman was asked whether he intended to open Sotheby's in his shopping centers, to which he categorically answered no. They asked him about his art collection, which he said was his own business, although he did say that he collected mainly twentieth-century paintings and Chinese antiquities. No one asked him how he was going to breathe new life into the firm. Nor did they ask him whether he was going to make any drastic changes. He reassured the staff that he would not be involved with the day-to-day operation and that he would make no changes until he had reviewed the present status. In the end, someone handed him the final question (all the questions had been written on pieces of paper, to protect the identity of the questioners).

"Is it true that you box every morning?"

As Taubman read the question aloud, a smile broke on his face and everyone laughed nervously. He looked around the room and said, "Yes, I do, when I am at home [in Michigan], which isn't often these days."

Later he learned who had asked the question. The boxer metaphor had gone very far in the biography of Alfred Taubman and he was pleased to have it perpetuated. Robert Wooley identified himself as the draftsman of the question. "Well, I'm glad you asked that one," Taubman said. "It lightened the atmosphere. The other ones were boring. That was a good one, Bob."

Little could Taubman have known that Wooley would later trot out the story for the benefit of the press, to which Taubman refused to speak during the gala party that evening. Nor could he have known that Robert was not known as Bob. In the Midwest, Roberts are often Bobs. He thought he had made it clear that there would be no interviews that night, even though the press was stationed above the stairwell as he entered looking very much like a victor, all but holding his hands over his head, as he had done when the Panthers won the game Marion lost money on, yelling out, "I love 'em. I love 'em," as his team raced in off the field.

Taubman had a lot to learn about the temperamental staff at Sotheby's. He was not so sure he liked this public position, although he allowed Westmorland to put his arm around him as a photographer took their picture together. Ford was more his style. Standing against another wall, the automobile mogul who was close to the royal family of Great Britain shooed the photographer away with a gruff "Beat it!" And then added, to make sure he got the point, "And I mean it. No pictures." Taubman had a lot to learn about the staff, but Taubman was a very quick study. In no time at all, he would stride confidently through the salesroom.

A week later Taubman showed up in another guise in another town. Having shucked his three-piece dark-blue business suit for an unusual black business suit set off by a lavender dress shirt and matching pocket square, the Svengali guided clients through the showplace Stamford Town Square in Stamford, Connecticut. The idea was to placate a restless group of retailers and government officials from Capitol South, a proposed Taubman Company shopping center two years overdue in Columbus, Ohio. And Taubman put on a showstopper act.

"Quality," he has said more than once, "takes time."

The group was duly impressed by the setup inside the mall. "It could be *Star Wars* . . . it could be Paris' Charles de Gaulle Airport . . . it could be Disneyland," *Connecticut Magazine* gushed on the opening of the shopping extravaganza, complete with reflecting pool and fountain that shoots an eighty-five-foot plume of water skyward, mirrored escalators that "glide like silent ribbons," elevators "as studded with lights as an amusement park ride" which "soar to the ceiling and descend into sunken pools."

SEVENTEEN

O UTSIDE the New Bond Street salesroom, a line of Daimlers and Rollses and Mercedeses as long as a funeral procession idled in strict formation on the narrow London street, their exhaust forming puffs of impatience in the cold December air.

The first annual meeting of the new board of directors of Sotheby's Holding Company, an American-based private corporation whose chairman is A. Alfred Taubman and vice-chairman is Henry Ford II, was under way inside the same mahogany-paneled second-floor boardroom where Cogan and Swid were frostily received exactly one year earlier. And if the fancy cars or bodyguards in burly huddles were any indication, the new board was very rich and very nervous. Along with Ford and Fisher, Taubman had invited leading lights from the world of international finance and private collecting, with close ties to major museums and department stores around the world.

Ann Getty, the wife of billionaire Gordon Getty and a collector in her own right, had joined the board, as had Baron Hans Heinrich Thyssen-Bornemisza de Kaszon, or Heinie. The baron is one of the richest industrialists in Europe and a private collector whose possessions are outnumbered only by those of the Queen of England, they say. He is also a close friend and business associate of Ford's. From Japan a rich department-store magnate, Seiji Tsutsumi, chairman of the Seibu Group —where Sotheby's held its first auction in the Far East some twenty years before—was asked to come aboard. Leslie Wexner, president of The Limited department stores and one of the richest men in the state of Ohio, had agreed to help his friend Taubman, too. As did Infanta Pilar, the sister of King Juan Carlos of Spain, and several others including Earl Smith, the former mayor of Palm Beach.

Everyone who follows the small and incestuous art circle had been wondering all fall what Taubman's first big move at Sotheby's would be. He had already installed an accountant, David Ward, to look over the books in London and New York— but that much was to be expected. There had been some problems with consignments in the fall, primarily because of speculation over Sotheby's future. The first of three installments of the much-coveted Florence Gould estate was snatched away by Christie's. Even though Wilson had said over and over that Florence, a neighbor and friend of his on the Riviera, "was a Sotheby's person," her trustees felt that there was too much "uncertainty" at Sotheby's to trust the house with her jewelry collection.

Wilson had been particularly upset by the loss. One of the few advantages of passing seventy, he had found, was that the friends he had turned into collectors over the years, like Gould, would sell off their estates through Sotheby's. He had been certain she would mention him and Sotheby's in her will. Alas, according to the trustees of the Florence J. Gould Foundation—the sole beneficiary of the auctions planned in three installments over the next few years—there was no mention of either party in her will. Christie's had simply come up with a better proposal. Taubman was upset, too, but not for personal reasons. He had never met Florence Gould, barely heard of her in fact. But he had heard from Wilson and others that her jewelry had been ogled by the Shah of Iran, who compared its sparkle to the Persian collection and valued it at up to $10 million.

There were other collections to be had. And Taubman was going to make sure Sotheby's had the edge over Christie's, at least outside Britain where Sotheby's has always led the pack anyway. This was why he had gathered together the group of swells who were meeting in private while their cars waited warmly for them outside. He had not excluded some members of the old board either. Lord Westmorland and Wilson, Thompson, Brunton, and Marion were present. Although no one would say what the board discussed for the first time, Marion indicated bluntly why they had been invited. Standing inside the vestibule of the Regency building (his wife, Mary Anne, by his side after a frantic hunt for a Cabbage Patch doll in London), he said: "Taubman has brought a whole bunch of rich people onto the board. They are going to find us things to sell."

The following day the dailies carried a brief news story listing the names of the new board members. Then the American press got wind of the names, and museum trustees began to tut-tut over the conflict of interest in the new board. The issue was hardly going to change the way Taubman did business, but it made for some rough sledding in the new year.

Taubman and Ford and Thyssen and Getty all sit on the boards of major museums. For obvious reasons, museums normally exclude those in the trade—dealers and auctioneers—from their boards. Museums being generally nonprofit public institutions that buy and sell works of art on a regular basis, the inclusion of a member of the trade in a museum's inner circle could raise questions about its nonprofit status and public support. Christie's and Sotheby's have in the past handled the issue by insisting that their directors resign from any museum or historic institution; only recently, Paul Ingersoll, who heads Christie's office in Philadelphia, was forced to give up his trusteeship at the Philadephia Museum of Art when he joined the auction house.

Taubman had neatly broken with the gentleman's tradition. And as could be expected, the injured parties behaved

gentlemanly. Taubman remained on the board of the Whitney.
Thyssen maintained his post at the Metropolitan Museum of Art.
None of the new trustees was asked to relinquish any museum
connection. And no museum asked any of them to step down,
either. Taubman had good reason to ignore the issue, although
he would not realize until later that the Whitney would bypass
Sotheby's in a sale of art to avoid appearing influenced by
Taubman. This upset him. For he had presumably seen the
museums as a rich source of material for sales. The museums
did not want to offend their trustees during the financially
troubled Reagan years, but they were skating on thin ice, since
too cozy a relationship could threaten their nonprofit status and
public support, and, like the Whitney, they had to give the appearance of fairness.

Should anyone have doubted that the art game had become a tough game under Taubman, all they would have needed
to do was walk through Sotheby's York Avenue salesroom. Where
once the pace seemed leisurely, almost lackadaisacal, the ultramodern offices now hummed with activity. And more than one
art expert mimicked a northern industrial accent as they formed
the words "Did you get the goods?" There was a certain prag-
matism to the Taubman approach. And there was a certain
urgency. In order to turn the loss-making operation into a profit-
making one, he would need to inject some hard salesmanship
into the phlegmatic staff. Fortunately, before too long Christie's would suffer a major setback in the presale festivities for
the auction of the Gould jewelry.

One of the great tributes to frippery, the Gould assembly
of diamonds and rubies and emeralds drew record crowds in
London, where the exhibition had begun a five-city tour in December 1983. Soon the crowds were storming St. James's, the
location of Christie's main salesroom. The popular press had
covered the story of the American millionairess and her fabled
jewels thoroughly. There were features in the *Sun*, *The Daily
Mirror*, and *The Star*; *The Daily Mail*, a paper that caters particularly to the social set in London, splashed pictures of Gould
and her jewels all over the inside cover. Even with less desir-

ables milling around the glass vitrines at the top of the grand stairwell, Christie's deferential crew handled each question politely. Unlike stuffy museums where no one can touch anything, visitors to Christie's and Sotheby's can actually handle the goods. The practice may seem to invite trouble, but the record of accidents and burglaries is amazingly brief, even in Britain, where armed guards are as rare as disorderly queues.

One American eyewitness said it was like the moment before a thunderstorm hits in the Great Plains. The patter of voices stopped abruptly, as though a radio had been turned off. Then the air seemed charged with a sort of electricity, and time stopped for the next few minutes. Stomachs dropped to knees and everyone hit the floor simultaneously, as though the whole affair had been carefully rehearsed beforehand.

There were three of them, all carrying sawed-off shotguns, American gangster-style. No one could identify them because their faces were squashed beyond recognition under stockings pulled tightly over their heads. No one moved or even seemed to breathe. In less than five minutes the crew smashed open a display case holding the most valuable of the gems and grabbed a diamond necklace worth millions and an earring worth nearly as much. A brave visitor slipped a necklace she had been admiring under her cape. Before the police arrived, the trio had fled with some of the finest pieces in the Gould collection. It was the first armed robbery in the 220-year history of Christie's.

But one robbery is one too many. In the beginning, some wanted to blame the Irish Republican Army, the radical terrorist group opposed to British occupation of Ulster, its first and last colony in Northern Ireland. Only weeks before, the IRA had been responsible for a car bomb attack on Harrod's during the height of the Christmas shopping season. But the IRA, which normally takes full credit for all attacks as a show of muscle and invincibility, never claimed the Christie's robbery for its own.

Had the IRA taken credit for the Christie's robbery, there would have been little need for a strong defense. A formidable opponent, able to strike almost any target without failure, the terrorist group is all but unstoppable, its depredations more a force of nature than a sign of the weakness of its victims. As it was, Christie's was left with quite a bit of explaining to do. The Gould trustees were understandably upset by the robbery and even went so far as to discuss calling the whole thing off. "There is one thing a trustee does not want to assume," Christie's president David Bathurst reflected afterward, "and that is the appearance of having acted irresponsibly with someone else's things."

Christie's, alas, convinced the trustees that security would be stepped up on all the planned stops for the jewelery over the next few months. The robbery turned out to be a blessing in disguise, for due to the perverse nature of human beings, even more people turned out to see the jewelry that was so valuable burglars wanted to steal it. But for Christie's fiduciary responsibility, the robbery remained a black mark and fodder for the opposition. Speaking of the Gould sales and why Sotheby's fared better in the end, David Nash, Sotheby's New York paintings director, later said, "There are many things trustees consider when they consign to an auction house. One of them is safety. Will the goods be safe? Will the goods be damaged or stolen? These are among the factors a trustee takes into account."

Sotheby's wasted no time getting to the Gould trustees. Days before the robbery, Marion had called the New York office of Gould's lawyer, John Young. Sotheby's had learned about the next installment before the rest of the world. El Patio, Florence's white elephant of a Spanish-style house on the beach in Cannes, bordered by the Mediterranean on one side and a railroad track on the other, had been sold before the trustees had intended. The new buyer, a French property developer, wanted to take possession immediately and the vast treasury had to be cleared out.

"Hello, Mr. Young, this is John Marion from Sotheby's."

"Hello. How are you?"

"I am fine, thank you."

"Good."

"Listen, I understand that you have sold the Gould place in Cannes."

"Well, yes. Yes, we have."

"You will probably need some help moving the furniture and her collections out. You know that our chairman emeritus lives in the area and was a close friend of hers, always said she was a Sotheby's person."

"Yes, I see. But wait a minute. How did you know about this? The sale only went through a few days ago. There was no announcement of it and we have not decided what to do about it yet."

"Someone intimate with the deal told me."

"Who?"

"One of our new directors."

"Who?"

"I am not at liberty to tell you. But as you may have heard, we have a new board of directors: Henry Ford, Ann Getty, Baron Thyssen . . ."

"Oh, yes, I believe I have."

"Well, we had our first meeting in London a few days ago and they told me about it then."

Marion wanted Young to give him the job of clearing out El Patio and selling the furnishings on the spot. This had happened before and there was no reason for him to believe Young would not give in to the bluff salesmanship that was Marion's forte. But Young seemed hesitant about the offer. Marion would not let up.

"John, we will go through the house and give you an appraisal immediately. I have a crew awaiting my go-ahead in New York and Paris. I will supervise the crew myself, along with Peter Wilson. We will move the furniture into a warehouse."

"Well, I appreciate your offer. That's very kind of you. But I cannot let this influence my thinking. We have the jewelry sale coming up and we all agreed that we would wait until that was over before we decided who would get the next installment. We must be thorough and impartial in this. We have a responsibility, you know."

"Of course you do. All I am offering is to give you a hand.

We are not going to charge you a thing for the service. It's just a friendly gesture."

"All right. Okay. Thank you. Go ahead with it, but remember that this will not influence our decision."

By the second week in January, Marion and his crew flew to Cannes to "get the goods," along with Wilson, who drove down from Clavary once again. Everyone knew that the Gould furniture and collection of *objets* were the least valuable and most labor-intensive installment of the three-part sale. Gould had a nose for rare jewels and good advice for her paintings, but her household furnishings were bought without discrimination, featuring leopard-skin-covered mediocre French furniture. Wilson would give her his standard "Oh, I *adore* that," but there was little reason for the experts to believe many others would agree.

The goal was not a valuable consignment, although the furnishings would eventually go for roughly $6 million, but "to get ourselves on the map with the trustees," as Marion put it simply. Within days the specialists had swept through the dusty rooms of El Patio. As macabre as the idea of sifting through a dead person's possessions seems to most of us, Sotheby's has worked out a system that is almost scientific. Expert A will hold up a candelabrum made at Sèvres in 1720. Expert B will note that a similar piece sold in London for $5,000. Without hesitation, A will place an estimate of $4,000 to $5,000.

Each expert is different. Some are morbidly fascinated by the setup, others come away deeply disturbed by the close contact with the dead. Two of the senior experts in New York once laughingly told a shocked gathering they were partners in Murder, Inc., a subsidiary of Sotheby's set up to help out during slow periods. Another expert who might be called Maurice confessed he had nightmares after going to work there. In his bad dream, a close friend had died. First he was ordered to sift through and appraise all the friend's possessions, including gifts he had given him over the years. Then he was told to recast the friend's life and turn him into a celebrity among the rich and famous, much as Sotheby's routinely does with people like Florence Gould. The poor expert became so troubled that he left Sotheby's.

Before Christie's even had a chance to see the Gould furnishings, Sotheby's had submitted a proposal to the trustees.
Young was a fair man, however. And he was not going to call a
vote on the matter until Christie's had a chance to submit a
proposal and to auction off her jewelry. Which they did with
great success in April in the main New York salesroom on Park
Avenue, the room that boasts a secret entrance into Regine's,
the disco of the jet set—most of whom seemed crammed into
the salesroom for a look at the action, a sea of perpetual suntans and a king's ransom in jewels. Bidding was fierce for the
Gould jewels, particularly for the Victory diamond, so called
because it was mined in South Africa the day the Allies claimed
victory in Europe. It fetched a record $2.7 million. Even Gould's
"traveling," or fake, jewels brought high prices. A pair of er-
satz diamond earrings was sold for $7,700, nearly four times
the generally accepted estimate. John Floyd, Christie's chairman and an Englishman of the old school who found Gould's
taste "gaudy," did little to arouse the excitement of the bidders, most of whom endured two hours of boredom for a few
minutes of avaricious thrills.

The main diversion came midway through the afternoon
session. As nearly everyone looked on in amazement, a party
made up of Gordon and Ann Getty, an unidentified male friend
dressed almost identically to Gordon in a dark wool Duke-of-
Windsor-style English double-breasted suit, and TV personal-
ity Barbara Walters traipsed down the main aisle during the
middle of a bidding battle. Nearly upsetting the contest, the
foursome marched some fifty feet through the audience, then
waited in the front while an attendant set up a special section
of folding chairs, providing ringside seats for the billionaire's
party. Within a few minutes the entourage attracted even more
attention. Without having placed a single bid, the Getty/Walters
party rose and swiftly departed the room, leaving everyone
wondering what had happened and why they had bothered to
come.

Alas, Getty and Walters probably realized they had stumbled into the wrong auction house. For over at Sotheby's there
was much more going on than a high-priced sale. Within a few

weeks the firm would announce the June sale in Monte Carlo of the contents of El Patio, a sale that the Gould trustees say Sotheby's won because Wilson was so familiar with Gould's taste and with the jet set on the Riviera, even though they had not considered this point important when assigning the jewelry to Christie's.

Within a few weeks, Taubman would begin to show what he had meant by bidding "at arm's length," at a sale of contemporary art in early May. Bidding for the De Koonings and Rothkos and Pollocks and Klines for sale this night was brisk. The contemporary art field, meaning art produced during or after World War II, is primarily an American market and competition between tycoons can be intense. Thyssen and Taubman, as well as Ford, Cogan, and Swid, all collect contemporary pictures, the field Llewellyn had dismissed as "not a big part of our business." But none of them was present in the room, at least in the beginning.

Suddenly Taubman walked casually past the press box, glancing over his shoulder as he picked a seat a few rows in front of one of New York's leading dealers who was bidding on a piece of sculpture. Without a moment's hesitation, Taubman joined in the contest. After twenty years of collecting, much of it through auctions, Taubman must have been aware of what he was doing. One of the cardinal rules of art dealing is: Never bid against a potential client. Which may explain why the dealer quickly stopped bidding, allowing Taubman to fight it out with an unidentified bidder calling in over the telephone. Finally Taubman withdrew his bid, and the piece was knocked down to the phone bidder.

The question is: Why was he challenging the system and how does his bidding handicap any opponent and jeopardize the seller's final price? He was presumably challenging the system because that is his style of operating, as he proved earlier when he went to museum boards for Sotheby's directors. It would appear that his bidding does handicap others because the owner of the place would hardly be expected to pay the 10 percent buyer's premium, although Taubman claims he does. This is a 10 percent advantage. The seller may or may not have lost money on this consignment, although it seems that the dealer bidding against Taubman was aware who his contestant was and withdrew presumably for that reason.

None of which really mattered. For the auction world is fairly unregulated in New York, falling under the jurisdiction of the Department of Consumer Affairs, which responds only to a rash of complaints from wronged consumers. Anyway, the thinking seems to go, this is rich man's game and let the rich police their own.

The May 1984 issue of *Town & Country*, the leading publication of what passes for upper class in the United States, said more than almost anyone could about the new status of the Taubmans, for there on the cover of the staid publication normally reserved for horsey debutantes out of St. Louis was Judy, dressed inside in nothing but a white bathing suit, lounging poolside in Palm Beach. Suzy Knickerbocker, the irrepressible society columnist, gave them a warm welcome to the world of New York, "where there are more candles and flowers than in the good old days in Versailles."

In London the Taubmans were another matter. Viewed cautiously at first, even as Sotheby's insisted he was really the true White Knight, the Taubmans stumbled during a luncheon hosted early in June after Peter Wilson's death. Like the Godmersham Park sale the year before, at which Judy got herself tangled in a battle against the Band-Aid heiress, Wilson's funeral, along with the Paris couture showings and the Gould sale in Monte Carlo, had been adopted this year as part of the American millionaires' summer circuit in Europe. Wilson died in Paris either of leukemia or diabetes, depending on which report is true, at the age of seventy-one, sadly before he had a chance to see any of Gould's prized possessions cross the auction block at Sotheby's or to benefit from the financial rewards that were probably due him from his years of courtship of Gould. At least one guest at the lunch felt that the Taubmans' jovial behavior was disrespectful, and before long London was abuzz with gossip about the two. Writing in *The Spectator*, a popular weekly, Taki

Theodoracopulos called him "the king of social mountaineer-ing," and her, "queen Judy."

Back in New York, the Taubmans conquered the Metropolitan Museum of Art, one of the pinnacles of the city's social moun-tain. One of the most elite preserves in New York, comprised of old money, like C. Douglas Dillon, former Secretary of the Treasury, its chairman at this time, the Met normally sends new money from Detroit shopping centers and fast food to the back of the line. And the line is not short. But only a year after Taubman made his grand entrance up Sotheby's stairwell as the White Knight, there he was again, hosting a benefit party for the museum with a glittering cast of characters rarely seen to-gether in the same room.

Sotheby's main salesroom was transformed into a tented pavilion with silver settings up for sale in the coming season. This was not strange to New Yorkers, accustomed to promotion and salesmanship as a way of life. For instance, there admiring the setup was Estee Lauder, five feet of shimmering jewels and makeup and one of Judy's closest friends and mentors.

"Isn't it beautiful!" Lauder said, clasping her hand over her mouth in awe. Suddenly an equally short man appeared by her side, looking severely agitated, gesticulating wildly.

"Come on, Essie." He implored her to stop gaping and move inside the tent. It was Jerry Zipkin, the man they call the moth because he is attracted to the brightest lights in society. On his heels was Roy Cohn. Bringing up the rear was Pat Buckley, the wife of conservative syndicated columnist William F. Buckley, Jr., and one of the tallest women on earth.

It was quite a party.

There was some flap in the papers that morning from the stuffier members of the WASP board, but never mind. There may have been some tut-tuts heard as Taubman handed Dillon a check for $50,000 and promised to match it. This was to be expected. "Why, it's like General Dynamics throwing a fund-raiser for the Pentagon," said one woman with close ties to Washington. "It just isn't done," said another.

EIGHTEEN

F OR the first time in the history of the firm, the attorney
general of the State of New York filed suit against Sotheby's
in September 1984. The charge was "persistent fraud and illegality," and the substance of the charge had been brought to
the attention of Attorney General Robert Abrams by a group
of Jewish leaders in New York City.

The leaders claimed that Sotheby's had acted wrongly in
an auction earlier in the year of a rare cache of Hebrew manuscripts and documents smuggled out of Nazi Germany in 1938.
The consignor did not have the right to sell the property, they
maintained. Moreover, Sotheby's had attempted to conceal the
fact that he had smuggled it from the Nazis, a very powerful
charge. The attorney general agreed with the complainants and,
after much deliberation with the auction house, finally pressed
the charges.

Sotheby's bristled, claiming that the attorney general, an
elected official, was politically motivated. The consignor, Dr.
Alexander Guttmann, the auction house contended, had the right
to sell the material. Guttmann, an eighty-year-old professor of
Talmudics at the Hebrew Union College in Cincinnati and a

survivor of the Holocaust, had been given the material by the officials of a Jewish seminary closed by the Nazis in 1941.

This was not the main issue. In charging *persistent* fraud and illegality, the attorney general's office was referring to the way in which Sotheby's had handled the announcement of the sale and subsequent follow-ups. Rather than tell interested parties that the material had been consigned by a survivor of the Holocaust and wrested out of Nazi Germany, the expert in charge originally claimed he did not know where the material had come from. The Jewish leaders claimed that this was the issue and, moreover, that Guttmann did not have the right to sell the material, "a very valuable document of Jewish persecution from the Middle Ages to the present, which belongs to the Jewish people."

Sotheby's was in a jam. Over the next ten months, at considerable legal expense, the lawyers would be forced to debate the law from more than one source, including German civil law, Nazi Restitution law, Jewish law, and American civil law. The expert claimed he had to protect the identity of the consignor. Taubman had nothing to do with the consignment or the alleged fraud, Sotheby's maintained. Which is probably true, the sale being a relatively small one in the overall scheme of Sotheby's day-to-day operations.

But there are those who would blame Taubman for the tone he set. His "get the goods" campaign had certainly helped the business, but it had also instilled some of the more frightened members of Sotheby's staff with a sense of "do or die," as one senior expert put it bluntly.

As the fall season dragged on without word from the trustees of the Florence J. Gould Foundation about the final installment of the Gould estate, the tension between Sotheby's and Christie's became less and less gentlemanly. Nash's remarks about trustees' considering whether goods will be stolen or damaged did not go unheeded over at Christie's. Bathurst, in fact, was in his office, complaining bitterly about Sotheby's move into the fast lane when Christie's suffered another mishap.

"David," his secretary said, looking unusually disturbed,

"there's been an accident. I think you should come and look immediately."

First it had been only a trickle through the second-floor ceiling of the Park Avenue salesroom. A few of the receptionists and uniformed porters held buckets and trays under the spouts issuing from Delmonico's Hotel on the third floor. By the time Bathurst barreled into the showroom, the trickle had grown to gusher proportions. Gallons of water were coming through the ceiling, in several good-sized waterfalls. The timing could not have been worse. For only a few feet away from the flood were millions of dollars' worth of Impressionist and modern paintings, put up for the gala opening party that November night, the preview for the major evening sale of the fall season. Fortunately none of the paintings was damaged and the flood was stopped and cleaned up by the time the first guests arrived.

The guests were to include the trustees of the Florence J. Gould Foundation, who had still not made up their minds who would auction the final segment of the estate, reportedly worth up to $150 million. The Cogans were also in the crowd that night, victors in another field. Marshall had recently purchased "21," the smart New York restaurant and remnant of the age of the three-martini lunch and men in gray flannel suits. Like Sotheby's, "21" was an institution in need of some brushing up, and Cogan, along with his ever-present partner Swid, intended to do it. They had paid a rather steep price for the moribund restaurant, too: $21 million. Not to lose track of the art market, Cogan had purchased the leading trade journal, *Art & Auction*, earlier in the year, and would soon host lunches at "21" for the art trade and press.

A few months later, Sotheby's unveiled its new marketing scheme on the front page of the Sunday *New York Times* business section. Taubman and his new president, Michael Ainslie, appeared brash, confident, and on top of something no one else had realized existed: a market for artworks that boasts an international annual turnover of $35 billion. With Sotheby's and Christie's combined turnover somewhere in the vicinity of $1 billion, there is no telling where they got the other $34 billion to make the total. Even the movie industry does not do $35 billion in business a year.

But there was more to the new Sotheby's approach to art sales than pie-in-the-sky figures. Taubman, who can sometimes sound as big as outdoors when he speaks, delivered one of his all-time classics in the same article. "Selling art," he said confidently, "is a lot like selling root beer. They are both something no one needs." Tell that to a thirsty youngster on a hot summer afternoon. ("What'll it be Johnny, a root beer or a Picasso?") The article was so full of new and unusual information about the art market that the official spokesmen for the firm were at a loss when asked about it in the days to follow. When asked how the $35 billion figure had been calculated, one senior spokesperson quipped, "I don't know. They probably multiplied the number of cans of root beer sold times the average price of a Picasso etching."

A few days later the Florence J. Gould Foundation consigned the final installment of the Gould estate to Sotheby's. By then, no one was particularly surprised by the decision, Sotheby's having pursued the consignment with a number of innovations that seemed once again to change the way art is sold. The main change was to isolate the sale and hold it at an otherwise quiet time of the year, late April, when no one would be distracted by the offerings in the traditional major May sales. Sotheby's also announced a new financing plan, whereby prospective buyers would be loaned up to 40 percent of the total hammer price. There was nothing new about negotiated loans, but there was something new about announcing the plan to the public, auction practices before Taubman having been more discreet and clubby.

More than anyone else, however, Sotheby's promised to pull out all stops with the Gould pictures. A special room with intense lighting was built for the pictures. Invitational lunches and drinks and dinners were held practically every day of the week. By the end of five months of intense partying, the bill for the frivolity-with-a-purpose would be estimated at $1 million, out of Sotheby's pocket. But all the promotion was needed. For the

Gould pictures were not worth anywhere near $150 million, at least after the French tax collectors finished picking through the best of them in lieu of death duties. Like Gould herself, the pictures were well framed and pretty, but aside from two, of little substance. They were worth at most $50 million according to initial reports, $10 million of which had been put on the Van Gogh landscape and $5 million on a Toulouse-Lautrec portrait, the two prizes.

Sotheby's went to work on the Gould legend too. Before long Florence Gould became known as "the greatest hostess in France" and "one of the leading patrons of French art." In Paris there was some outcry in the press—not because of who Sotheby's had said she was, but because of the mediocre quality of the paintings overall. GOULD SALE SETS NEW RECORD—FOR HYPE, Sourien Milikian blasted in the *International Herald Tribune*. In London, *The Times* reported with a sniff that her pictures were "made to go with the furniture."

"Everyone wanted to get into her house," John Marion said, in front of a gathering in the specially designed salesroom lit with lamps that made both people and pictures look better.

"Yes," someone quipped. "Wasn't she robbed a few times?"

The café society crowd was remarkably absent the evening of the Gould sale. Even though Taubman had had specially designed boxes, like those at the opera, installed around the room, he could not lure the society set into the salesroom. They probably knew better, Gould having been a member of their parents' or their parents' parents' set. There were not even any actors or actresses, as there had been at the Havemeyer sale two years before. Instead there were faces "remarkably new to us," according to Sotheby's face spotters, and bidding with borrowed money, it seemed, lent by the new Sotheby's.

For the first ten minutes or so the bidding was remarkably slow, with many lots failing to meet their lower estimated value— some not selling at all. Then the Van Gogh circled in front of the audience. *"Paysage au Soleil Levant,"* or "Landscape with Rising Sun," had been painted in 1889 shortly after the artist committed himself to a mental hospital at St. Rémy in the South of France. In a swirl of brilliantly hued colors, Van Gogh captured the field and sunrise outside his window in the asylum. "It is like a picture of a vision one has never seen," his brother Theo wrote to him. "One day I hope my paintings will be worth what I have spent on paint," a disturbed Vincent wrote back to his brother.

Then the bids began to come up. First in fifty-thousand-dollar increments, then in hundred thousands, quickly passing a million dollars, then two, three, five, six, with a prolonged pause at seven million dollars. Marion looked nervously out at the audience and glanced furtively to the box where Taubman was seated, next to the box where the trustees looked down at the spectacle. No one could see where the bids were coming from, although some had been placed over the telephone hookups in the front of the room. The bidding began again, slowly edging upward in what could only be called a tug-of-war between two equally matched opponents, whoever they might be. Finally the bidding paused again at nine million dollars, a million shy of the promised ten-million-dollar record which had been set at Christie's a few days before in the sale of a rare painting by Andrea Mantegna, the fifteenth-century northern Italian master. Once, twice, three times, Marion looked around the room at the assembled big spenders.

Sold!

In the post-sale scramble to discover who bought what, the identity of the purchaser of the Van Gogh at $9.9 million (including the 10 percent buyer's premium) was a mystery. Original reports suggested that Stavros Niarchos, the Greek shipping magnate, had bought it. But then another name surfaced in the press. The picture, according to the *International Herald Tribune*, had been purchased by A. Alfred Taubman. Taubman quickly denied having bought the Van Gogh, although one of the trustees claimed that he had been told Taubman would buy it if no one else did. The mystery of the buyer had still been unsolved by the end of the summer of 1985, by which time Taubman had yet another tale of Christie's woes to gloat over.

David Bathurst had resigned during the summer after he was found guilty by the Consumer Affairs Department of "lying in a 1980 sale." Bathurst had told the press that a picture had sold when in fact it had not. This, the department concluded, had created a "false market" for, coincidentally, paintings by Van Gogh. Taubman pointed out at smart dinners that this sort of thing never happened at Sotheby's.

Months after the sale of the Van Gogh, when names would usually surface through the small and fastidious art grapevine, the only name on the list was still Taubman's. Writing in *Manhattan Inc* in September 1985, Michael Thomas reported that he believed Taubman had bought the picture. If he did, he would surely have unloaded the picture by then. One of the many advantages of investing in artworks, as the naysayers failed to recognize when Taubman paid too much for Sotheby's, is the flexibility an art investment carries. As Thyssen, Ford, Getty, Wilson, and others have long since learned, artworks, unlike any other investment, carry no papers and can be easily moved across national boundaries, even carrying fair title into Switzerland and Monte Carlo.

Or in the case of the elusive Van Gogh perhaps into the Buenos Aires home of cement millionairess Amalita Fortabat. At first she denied the picture was hers, telling *Vanity Fair*'s Bob Colacello, teasingly, "Maybe Alfred Taubman bought [the Van Gogh] and doesn't want to say." Fortabat, a woman who has been known to spend millions on art and jewelry, was reputed to have been the underbidder in the original auction.

Whatever the initial advantages of Sotheby's for Taubman, by the end of his second year behind the podium they must have seemed meager. The auction, one of the last vestiges of unfettered free enterprise, was suddenly under attack from at least two government agencies. The bottom line continued to plague the British institution; and, in fact, during the summer of 1985 overhead costs were cut once more: Graham Llewellyn, James Lally, and no fewer than fifty others were let go in a money-saving measure.

At least one of Sotheby's goals had been more or less achieved. The competition, in the wake of Bathurst's resignation, was worn down by the scandal. This may not have been exactly what Wilson meant when he predicted that one day there would be room for only one auction house. In October, despite the new austerity campaign, Taubman appointed Lord Gowrie as chairman of the board, a job he himself had previously held, at what insiders report to have been a very competitive salary. Gowrie, former Minister of Arts for Great Britain, had been widely rumored as a replacement for Bathurst's place at Christie's.

This time it was Christie's turn to feel the heat of shareholder dissatisfaction. By early fall 1985 the share price had dropped precipitously and then began to climb mysteriously once again, a sure sign some take-over action was afoot. Cogan noticed this drop and pointed out, jokingly, that perhaps Christie's could use some help, which Sheikh Nasser al-Salem al-Sabah, a member of the enormously rich ruling family of Kuwait, seemed unwilling to supply. Only adding to the confusion were the rumors that Sotheby's too was up for sale once again. Only this time there would be no wholly unacceptable suitors or gleaming white knights to save the day, Taubman having closed the chapter on proxy battles when he removed the firm from the public market.

Many still insist Taubman bought Sotheby's to please his new bride. There is no doubt it was the perfect present for someone like Judy. In September 1985 she used the dealing rooms for yet another foray in the world of the rich and famous. This time she hosted a *durbar* in the presence of Her Royal Highness The Duchess of Gloucester. A *durbar* is not a muffin, but rather an Anglo-Indian feast, complete with tributes of fealty to the reigning monarch. Since Judy was the only untitled name on the original invitation, a few began to wonder where the tributes should be sent.

As Cyril Connolly once said about someone very different, Judy Taubman was last seen illuminated by "a blaze of names":

Their Graces The Duke and Duchess of Devonshire
Their Graces The Duke and Duchess of Marlborough
Their Graces The Duke and Duchess of Wellington
The Most Honourable The Marchioness of Dufferin and Ava

The Right Honourable The Viscount De L'Isle

The Right Honourable The Viscount Norwich

His Excellency Sir Oliver Wright, G.C.M.G., G.C.V.O., D.S.C.,
    Her Britannic Majesty's Ambassador, and Lady Wright

His Excellency Sir John Thomson, G.C.M.G., the United King-
    dom Permanent Representative to the United Nations, and
    Lady Thomson

Sir Hugh and Lady Casson

Mick Jagger and Jerry Hall

INDEX